A place to begin building memories
for the future . . .

MountainStar 2004

Patterns *of* Home

Patterns of Home

THE *Ten* ESSENTIALS OF ENDURING DESIGN

Max Jacobson

Murray Silverstein

Barbara Winslow

The Taunton Press

The Taunton Press

Inspiration for hands-on living™

The Taunton Press, Inc., 63 South Main Street, PO Box 5506, Newtown, CT 06470-5506
e-mail: tp@taunton.com

Distributed by Publishers Group West

JACKET DESIGN: Susan Fazekas
INTERIOR DESIGN AND LAYOUT: Susan Fazekas
ILLUSTRATOR: Martha Garstang Hill (principal) and JSW Architects

Library of Congress Cataloging-in-Publication Data
Jacobson, Max, 1941–
    Patterns of home : the ten essentials of enduring design / Max Jacobson, Murray Silverstein, Barbara Winslow.
        p. cm.
    ISBN 1-56158-533-5
    1. Architecture, Domestic--Designs and plans. 2. Architectural design--Technique. I. Silverstein, Murray. II. Winslow, Barbara. III. Title.
    NA7115 .J334 2002
    728' .37'0222--dc21
                                        2002007103

Printed in the United States of America
10 9 8 7 6 5 4 3 2 1

ACKNOWLEDGMENTS

Many people have helped us with this book, and we take this opportunity to offer our thanks. First and foremost, we would like to express our gratitude to the extraordinary staff at The Taunton Press. In particular, many thanks to our superb editor, Peter Chapman, who guided us so gracefully from conceptualization through final draft; to Jim Childs, for his vision and steady support; to Paula Schlosser, our marvelous art director, for giving the book such an elegant and appealing look; to Susan Fazekas for her work on the design and layout; to illustrator Martha Garstang Hill; and to design manager Carol Singer. Special thanks to Chuck Miller, editor of *Fine Homebuilding* magazine, for helping us formulate the project and encouraging us along the way.

Much of the vitality of architectural books comes from their photography. Photographer David Livingston criss-crossed the country shooting the featured houses, and we are grateful for his amazing capacity to both understand what we were after and bring it to life with his fluid technical skill.

To the homeowners of all the houses portrayed in the book, a warm thanks for letting us photograph and write about your homes. Thanks also to the architects whose work is included for submitting material and helping us to understand it; and to the architects and their clients who submitted inspiring projects that, within the scope of a single volume, we simply were not able to use. We are particularly indebted to Sarah Susanka, who helped us find our way to many of the architects whose work we have had the good fortune to study.

Deep thanks to Chris Alexander and the Center for Environmental Structure in Berkeley, California. From 1967 to 1974, Max and Murray worked at the Center; and along with Chris, Sara Ishikawa, Shlomo Angel, Ingrid King, and Denny Abrams, they helped create the 1977 book *A Pattern Language*. *Patterns of Home* draws on our experience as practitioners at JSW Architects, but its foundations lie in the work begun at the Center by these people.

We could not have written this book as we did—in the middle of our office, in the midst of a busy practice—without substantial help from an unusually talented and supportive staff. Thanks to everyone in the office during the time the book was occupying our attention. In particular, thanks to Helen Degenhardt, Doug Shaffer, and Robert Fukuda for reviewing chapters and offering comments; to Tran Nham and Priscilla Thomas for helping us track down the architects from all over the country who submitted work; and to Brydie McPherson, for copy editing several chapters and taking on the task of credits and permissions with such wonderful energy and good spirit.

CONTENTS

Twenty-five years ago a book was published that precipitated a paradigm shift in the way we understand the built environment. *A Pattern Language* made residential architecture, building design, and city planning much more accessible to people not trained in the field. Its goal was to put the tools for making great places back into the hands of those who use them, by explaining the underlying patterns of behavior and form that shape experience. That book was assembled by a group of architects and architecture students who pooled their insights to arrive at some 250 patterns that affect the way we live. The book provided an extraordinary contribution to design philosophy, but its shear scope and scale made it a daunting prospect for all but the most dedicated of readers.

Two of the original authors, Max Jacobson and Murray Silverstein, along with Barbara Winslow, their partner in architectural practice, now offer a new and far more manageable volume, featuring the ten most critical patterns for residential design. Although each pattern seems deceptively simple, the application of each of these ideas can transform a house into a far more evocative place to live— one of integrity and substance, as the projects used to illustrate each admirably demonstrate. Best of all, because the authors have spent most of their professional lives using and evolving the patterns, they bring a breadth of knowledge that gives the reader access to a quarter century of refinement of the original notions.

Whether or not you are planning to build or remodel a house in the near future, this book will give you much insight into why certain houses seem to resonate with the lives of their inhabitant while others seem lacking. As you'll see from the pages that follow, none of this is particularly complicated. It simply results from careful observation of what our senses tell us about the places we inhabit. *Patterns of Home* gives back to the homeowner the tools to make a house a truly wonderful place to live.

—*Sarah Susanka*
Raleigh, North Carolina
August 2002

Years ago, at the beginning of our professional careers, two of us were part of an effort to create a design language that was similar in many ways to what we are now calling "the patterns of home." In that work, *A Pattern Language* (Oxford University Press, 1977), we and our colleagues at the Center for Environmental Structure in Berkeley defined over 200 design ideas, which we called patterns.

In a general sense, patterns are a designer's rules of thumb, the intuitive principles, often unspoken, that guide design work. And just as our innate knowledge of grammatical rules allows us to speak fluently and create well-formed sentences, an architect's innate sense of patterns allows him or her to design fluently, to create well-formed buildings. In *A Pattern Language,* our emphasis was on patterns that grew directly out of the way people use and experience buildings, dealing with such issues as how to create balanced natural light in a room, how to create a graceful flow of circulation through rooms, and how to organize a building to make comfortable outdoor spaces around it. The book contained our deepest intuitions and understandings about what makes buildings work, what makes them good to be in.

A Pattern Language was an important step, but it was not a building. As young architects, above all we wanted to build. Living in the Bay Area, we found ourselves surrounded by buildings that brilliantly embodied many of the patterns we had tried to define, inspiring and inventive houses by Bernard Maybeck, Greene and Greene, Julia Morgan, Charles Moore, Joe Esherick, William Turnbull, and many others. Hungry to put ideas into practice, we found a client and, in 1974, began a residential design practice that, combined with teaching at local colleges and universities, has remained the focus of our professional lives. The years of practice and teaching have taught that, while many of the original patterns retain intuitive appeal "light on two sides," "entrance transition," and "farmhouse kitchen" are a permanent part of our design language—many others have come to seem unwieldy or overstated or are simply irrelevant to the kinds of problems we have faced. And while it seems to us that the original notion—that good houses are made of deep, traditional patterns, grounded in human experience—is still valid, practice has made us realize that the really crucial patterns are far fewer in number than we had previously thought; and that this smaller group of patterns is more powerful than we had previously imagined.

THE CRITICAL PATTERNS

We can put this another way: While there may be many dozens, even hundreds, of patterns that go into the making of homes, there are only a handful that we would now say are essential. And further, these few essential patterns are more tightly clustered and inter-related than we had understood. When they are used successfully, they are like facets of a single thing, inextricably bound together, working in concert to produce the feelings that we associate with home.

When we sat down with our notes for this book, we each took a stab at defining the various patterns that seemed to us most valuable—the critical patterns of home design that you must get right. We were surprised to find that we each came up with a similar handful and that they easily and clearly merged into a group of ten. As we talked with other architects and designers about "our ten," we began to see that, although everyone would parse it out a little differently, we all seemed to be talking about the same cluster of ideas, the same underlying phenomena.

It may be that trying to come up with a perfect list of this sort is impossible: The patterns of home are

never, finally, the home. Good buildings are always more than the patterns they embody. Wonderful homes always instruct us anew on the power of natural light on a wall, the truth of materials, the pleasures of outdoor rooms, the proportions of height to width in rooms, the sense of arrival, the feeling of shelter and refuge.

Even so, making the attempt to define the patterns and how they work to create a satisfying building raises our level of understanding; gives language to our experience; and may, in the end, make us better designers.

In the chapter that follows we introduce the ten patterns and some of the buildings we have selected to embody them. This introductory chapter is followed by the heart of the book: ten chapters that tackle the patterns one by one and show them at work in a variety of ways. Each of the ten pattern chapters features two or more homes that we think provide strong illustrations of the pattern in question.

Like all well-designed things, good homes do many things at once. They embody many more of the patterns than the one being illustrated in a given chapter. A home that is well related to its site, that makes its outdoors into wonderful rooms, will no doubt also be good at capturing light, creating lively spaces in the "seam" between indoors and out, and so on. We make this clear by highlighting those aspects of the featured homes where there is a strong concentration of patterns; where, by virtue of good design, they are doing many things at once; and where the patterns are working together to illuminate our understanding of *home*.

DISCOVERING THE ESSENCE OF HOME

A private place of refuge and outlook has been created at the edge of a family room.

The gabled dormer rising from the broad roof centers the entry below and announces "home."

DESIGNING A NEW HOME, or significantly changing an existing home, is a process of discovery. Like explorers, architects and their clients work together to discover a new place. And even though, as professional architects, we have designed many new homes and additions for a great variety of owners and sites and budgets, each time we start, it feels as if we are charting a new course, seeking a new place, one that neither we nor our clients have seen before.

It is a somewhat paradoxical process, for when we "arrive"—the project successfully done, the residents settled in—the owners often feel that the new place is familiar, a place they already know. "Yes," they say, "this is what we had in mind."

Creating a home is a process of making a place that feels both new and old: new, in so far as it is a fresh response to the existing conditions of neighborhood, site, climate, program, and budget; and old, in that it contains the deep and familiar qualities that, regardless of location, budget, and size, make a place a home. These timeless architectural qualities are what we think of as the essence of home.

DNA FOR HOME

Just as individuals share common genetic material, it seems likely that we possess a shared sense of the essence of home. It is based on our deepest spatial instincts; on our common experience of gravity; on our dependence as infants; on our two-legged uprightness; on our needs for sun, refuge, and place; on our desires for being alone and being together; and on our quest for order and variety.

Think of places you've known that feel good—comfortable, balanced, dynamic, alive—and then try to derive from such places the qualities and characteristics they share. This is what architects do as a matter of course, as they recall favorite places, meet with clients to plan a project, design and experience the homes that result, visit buildings they admire, and note their mistakes and successes over the years.

Over a career of working on housing and homes, architects develop an instinctive sense for the basic pattern, the underlying order that defines a home; and each project, though it requires the patient work of new discovery, is also a process of applying this underlying pattern, manifesting it anew, learning another of its infinite forms.

The house engages the site. Living in the house, we inhabit the site.

THINKING IN PATTERNS

The essence of home is a notion that, while hard to describe abstractly, seems to be understood intuitively. We all have a sense of the spaces and places that possess it: entries that invite, kitchens that work and are a pleasure to be in, rooms that feel right, and those that, somehow, don't. And while such things are, of course, subjective—a matter of taste, preference, desire—beneath the varieties of taste and style, there is a definable underlying *essence* that can be embodied in a wide variety of homes—big and small, traditional and modern.

So how do we capture this essential quality to create houses that are memorable, satisfying, and enduring? After designing hundreds of houses ourselves, we have come to believe that the key is to apply a group of design concepts—what we call *patterns*—that focus on the experience of being in a home. Buildings designed using this approach can be of any style, fit any site, suit any size family or budget. The patterns can be used to evaluate existing buildings, to help plan remodels, or to guide a design from the ground up. They are the essential tool for anyone intending to buy, build, or remodel a home—and a dreamer's guide for those whose plans are just beginning.

WHAT IS A PATTERN?

We are all familiar with patterns in our daily lives. We use them to create meals (recipes, menu plans, cooking guides), to make clothes (sewing patterns), and generally to organize our approach to solving a problem. They are the tools that we count on to help us through a new experience, and they can become so familiar and natural that we use them intuitively, no longer having to think before we act. In its simplest form, a pattern is an idea about how something is done. At its best, a pattern can distill the wisdom of the past, reveal the potential of the future, and link with other patterns to form a language to guide a process. Patterns help us consider the essential elements as we undertake the creation of something new or the evaluation of something old. Designing with patterns does not lead to a preconceived result but to an infinite variety of solutions based on the specific conditions.

Don't people already know what they want in a house? Well, yes—sort of. There's certainly a vocabulary in use to produce houses, and most of us understand it easily—three bedrooms, two baths, sunken tub, formal dining room, grand entry. But the language used to talk about houses is too often one that focuses on resale value or curb appeal; it is a language of real estate rather than experience. The *patterns of home* go deeper, linking the way the house is designed with the way we experience the world. They explore the presence of light, the way we move through a space, the feel of one space as you are sitting in another, the relationship of indoors and outdoors.

Good homes reveal themselves gradually containing qualities of both order and mystery.

Think of the house and its site as a single thing but also as parts shaped by a larger environment.

A house reaches out to its site,
creating rooms outside as well as in.

THE ESSENTIAL PATTERNS OF HOME

From our experience as designers and teachers, we have distilled ten patterns, or design concepts, that form the essence of home. In the chapters that make up the heart of this book, each pattern is explored, one by one, with the help of built examples. But first let's introduce them.

We present the patterns in an order that starts with the site and the most basic concerns of site planning and ends with the selection of building materials. This order is one way to think through a design. It should be noted, however, that there is no real scale to the patterns—the first can be used to focus on details of plants and paving; the last can be used to think about the building as a whole and its relationship to its site and its neighbors. Any one of the patterns can be a starting point, a point of departure, for beginning a design.

PATTERN ONE

Inhabiting the Site

Think of the house and its site as a single thing but also as parts shaped by a larger environment. The site is a part of a larger place—a neighborhood, a ridge, a region—and the house itself, no matter how large and complex, is a part of this larger order. In some sense, the house must participate in the larger whole: a whole that includes views; the path of the sun; the presence of neighbors, sound, sidewalks, and roads; the nature of the soil; the places that are good to be in just as they are; the ugly places; the places in between. Getting the feel and sense of the site, finding the order latent in the site, placing the house to preserve and relate to the best of the site—all this is achieved in the first pattern, Inhabiting the Site. Get it right, and the rest of the design will flow smoothly.

Creating Rooms, Outside and In

Buildings give shape to their interior spaces but also to the exterior spaces around them. Imagine the site as containing a mosaic of rooms, some inside and some out. The walls and wings of the house, as well as the paths and features of the site, define these rooms. Think of the outdoor rooms of the site as every bit as positively formed and invested with meaning as the indoor rooms. Identify the best outdoor places and use the elements of the building to help define them. If you don't plan the house to shape rooms both outside and in, the outdoor rooms will end up as leftover spaces. Similarly, the indoor rooms will lack the coherence of design and feel detached from the site if they are organized without attention to the interplay of in and out. In a well-designed house, there is a lively balance of indoor and outdoor rooms, and the two types of spaces make an interlocking quilt of the site.

A roof is more than a cap on top of a building; it is the fundamental space out of which the form of the building develops.

As much as walls and floors and ceilings, natural light gives shape and life to space. Good homes capture light—filter it, reflect it—in ways that, no matter the season or time of day, delight their inhabitants.

Sheltering Roof

One of the defining comforts of home is the feeling of being enveloped by a simple, sloping roof. The primitive house was essentially a roof on the ground, which speaks to the very essence of home. More than any other single element, the form of the roof—as experienced both outside and in—carries the look and meaning of shelter, of home. The overall roof plan, how it orients and shapes the spaces below and around it, how the parts of the roof are linked, the details of roof construction and how they will be expressed inside and out… all form the pattern Sheltering Roof. For a house to convey the meaning of home, its roof must be more than something tacked onto the rest of the building. It must express how the house is inhabited. The most powerful houses are those in which, in some form, the whole building is conceived as a sheltering roof.

Capturing Light

A sheltering roof is primarily a defense against weather, but a home must also open itself to the light and warmth of the sun. Arrange interior spaces to gather light, each according to its needs, over the course of a day and over the course of the seasons. Important rooms deserve balanced light from at least two sides. And try to let light surprise you somewhere: a drop of light on a landing, a wash of light on a north wall. Above all, use natural light and the forms employed to collect it—windows, dormers, skylights, monitors, and wells—to reinforce the order of the plan: The important centers, edges, paths, and goals are all revealed by Capturing Light.

Parts in Proportion

A home is an assembly of parts, materials, and spaces—entry, roof, garage, kitchen, bedroom—and, in some graceful, rhythmic way, all these parts must add up to an orderly and sensible whole. What *are* the major parts going to be? How big will they be? How will they contain or support the minor parts? Is the building a sequence of parts, strung together like beads on a necklace; one overall form, a center with appendages; a great suitcase packed with minor parts; or something in between? Each element is both a part of something larger and a whole with its own constituent parts: A wall is part of a room or wing but also a whole that contains windows, which contain sashes, which contain glass, which contain divisions (called muntins). A home is a hierarchy of Parts in Proportion and will feel comfortable only when all its parts are in good proportion to each other and make up a balanced whole.

All the parts of this space—windows, walls, post, beam—unite in a hierarchy of good proportion.

WORKING WITH A PATTERN

When a chef sets out to make, say, a chopped salad, she may have one of several recipes in mind (Cobb, Waldorf, and so on). But as she works, she will draw on certain rules of thumb (chop so each forkful contains a bit of everything; balance salty with bitter) that are deeper than the recipe and that make all the difference to the quality of the finished dish. The patterns of home are like the chef's rules of thumb: They are spatial rules, deeper than regional or historical style, that apply to any home and determine its qualities as a place.

Take the simple example of getting adequate light into a room. We know that if we can bring light into a space from two directions, instead of just one, the room will almost certainly feel bright and well lit. Similarly, if light enters the room from windows on only one wall, the room will likely feel unpleasant, with the window area too bright and the rest of the room too dark and shadowy. Thus the power of the simple formula "Light a room from two sides" is one of the key guidelines for the pattern Capturing Light. Once we grasp this pattern, we can use it to design a new room or to help diagnose the quality of natural lighting in an existing room with an eye toward remodeling.

Finding the right mix of common and private spaces is one of the key issues of good design.

Neither out nor in, this house forms along its exterior edge a wonderful place in between.

The Flow through Rooms

How we arrive on a site and how we enter the house and move through it have profound influences on our sense of the building as home. Walk onto the site in your mind's eye and head toward the entry; find the places where you naturally pause, walk through the front door and pause again; continue to walk through the house, coming and going. The entire sequence of movement through and around the house determines whether we feel welcomed, invited to move farther, or encouraged to linger at a threshold, settled and comfortable within a space. Movement through a room affects the room itself. Whether or not a room—a house!—feels settled and comfortable is directly related to *how* we move through it.

Private Edges, Common Core

Against the flow of movement, rooms are meant to hold activity, to gather and focus the life of the home. Some of this activity is shared, like two people cooking together or a family playing a game of cards; some of it is private, like reading a book. A good home balances private and communal space throughout. It offers magnetic and lively centers, reinforced by light and ceiling shape, with circulation at the edges; and it provides claimable private areas for everyone, even if the spaces are tiny (private niches, desks, window seats, and alcoves). Some spaces are exclusively common, some exclusively private; but most often good rooms are a subtle mixture of the two. Finding the right mix of common and private spaces is one of the key issues of good design.

Private Edges, Common Core is a pattern that can be applied at many scales. Here, on the scale of a dining room, the fireplace helps define the common room and, at the same time, forms a private niche off of it.

The instinct to create a place that is both protected and yet contains a broad overlook is one of our deepest spatial needs.

Refuge and Outlook

One of the abiding pleasures that homes offer is being in and looking out—providing a solid, stable, and protected place from which you can look out toward and over a larger "beyond." Think of how this drama can be enacted on the site—in both major and minor, social and private ways: caves with views, inglenooks open to larger rooms, carved-out terraces looking out on a distant view. Think about perches, playhouses, alcoves, and window seats: solid backs and open fronts. In all cases, the core of the experience is being able to observe the outer world comfortably from a position of relative security. Usually, the refuge is at a higher position and is enclosed and dark—the outlook is normally below, unenclosed, and light. At its simplest, we are inside looking out.

Places in Between

The house on its site makes up a series of indoor and outdoor rooms. But many spaces are neither inside nor outside; they are in between. And it is this in between-ness that makes them so permanently appealing. The traditional front porch, carved into the mass of the house, is the archetypal place in between. But such places can be imagined and found throughout a home: bay window seats and beds, balconies, sleeping porches, breezeways, gazebos, summer rooms, rooms with walls that disappear. Just as important as a home's indoor and outdoor places are its Places in Between, places that allow you to inhabit the edge, that offer enough exposure to make you aware of your surroundings, and that provide just enough protection to make that awareness comfortable.

Composing with Materials

Finally, a home is not just something of the mind and the imagination. It must be built; *made* of something: made of materials. Choosing its materials—to support, frame, fill, cover, color, and texture space—is the act of composing the home. There are many decisions to be made: What are the major materials? How are they expressed and experienced? What materials will establish the fundamental themes? What kinds of rhythms, repetition, variation will be played out around and within the home? Columns, overhangs, soffits; beams, smooth white planes, thickness. Putting materials together in a way that promotes their individual qualities, longevity, and visibility is the art of composing with materials. Compose materials as a melody—those that support and underscore; those that offer counterpoint, slow the progression—all with a view to letting the building sing.

The exposed ceiling framing provides a sense of rhythm and order for this space.

This room is balanced by the fireplace—designed to center and anchor the room—and by the glass wall, which lets it expand out into the distance.

This couple's bedroom is formed as a small private place of refuge within a roof dormer at the edge of the house. The dormer is opened up to create an outlook, with French doors that open out on a balcony. A glazed arch captures light and echoes the curve of the eyebrow dormer on the other side of the roof. Five of the patterns are at work in this one space: Sheltering Roof; Capturing Light; Parts in Proportion; Private Edges, Common Core; and Places in Between.

THE WAY THE PATTERNS WORK TOGETHER

It should be clear that the set of ten patterns we have selected is somewhat arbitrary—both in number and inclusion. Other architects might settle on a group of eight; some might add a few patterns. But from our experience with refining this list and presenting it to others, we feel certain that, plus or minus, we have staked out the essential ground and have named a group of patterns that form the core of what is required to make a wonderful home.

In any case, before investigating the patterns individually, we want to pause and emphasize that it is *the way they work together* that makes all the difference in a house design. The patterns are isolated and given separate discussion only because books must be made of discrete chapters and because this allows us to focus on manageable ideas and elements as we design. In truth, however, the patterns are all parts of a larger whole. (You'll notice throughout the book that we've included "Patterns in Context" boxes to draw attention to houses that showcase several patterns working together.)

Consider an example. A master bedroom is a space for a couple, a couple's *realm*, which includes both shared and private spaces. If you were thinking of adding a master bedroom to your home, you might begin by reading PRIVATE EDGES, COMMON CORE, where you would find examples of spaces and principles that could be applied to the design of a master bedroom. But as soon as you begin to imagine the bedroom, you begin to think about how it will be located and shaped to capture light and view, how to make it a place of refuge, how it relates to or creates outdoor rooms, and what materials it will be made of and how can they be used to express the meaning of the space: intimacy, retreat, quiet, morning light, relationship to children's room, and so on. In effect, a small group of patterns quickly comes

together and defines the preliminary design of the project: the master bedroom as a common space with the capacity to sustain private activities; a place of refuge with a private view; a place that is located and organized to capture morning light.

The patterns can be used to raise questions, to evaluate ideas, to enrich our ability to think conceptually about new projects. In the case of the master bedroom, natural light can be captured and used to center the place for the bed—or not. The sense of refuge can be created by low ceilings, which can be used to intensify the intimacy of the space—or not. The edges of the room can be thickened to create private work spaces for each person—or not. In one way or another, the decision to work with one pattern inevitably pulls up several others in its train, creating a sequence of design opportunities, as one pattern works to reinforce and augment another.

The way the patterns work together is illustrated by the diagram at right, which shows each as an identifiable component of a larger structure. The lines of connection between patterns might be drawn differently by different designers and depend on the particular project. We want only to illustrate the *fact* of interconnection: The patterns form a field, and a given design project will fire off connections between them, similar perhaps to what goes on in the synapses of the brain as creative work goes forward.

From the exterior, the master bedroom dormer helps to "cap" the roof and give a center and proportion to the rear of the house.

The ten patterns may be thought of as working together to form a single organic whole. But any given project, as it evolves, will highlight small clusters of patterns within this framework.

PATTERNS IN HARMONY

As an example of the way the patterns work together to produce a timeless home, let's look at a house that we remodeled in northern California. The house was originally built as a family home but had served for many years as a convent. The interiors had been divided into many small rooms—cells, bedrooms, and chapel—all turned inward; and the common spaces were minimal and stark. But, as the Realtors say, the

A few patterns cluster and form a template, a flexible interrelated set of ideas that, like the grammatical rules of a language, work together to produce the underlying structure of home.

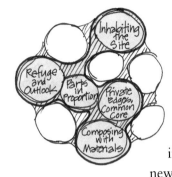

building had great bones. And our clients loved the location, the view, and the original brown shingle style of the building. They could see something archetypal in the house, something that made them feel that the old building would make a wonderful new home. Could we help them find that something in the essence of the old house and bring it to life in a new/old home?

Compared to many remodeling projects we have done, this one was complex, requiring new work at every level, from foundation to roof. We developed a program, listing the number, size, and kinds of spaces the owners wanted; assembled a team of consultants, contractor, and subs; and produced a bulky set of technical drawings. But in the end, reflecting back on this home, we were struck by the fact that a few simple design ideas seemed to matter most—organizing the house to capture natural light, making the dead attic space under the old roof a vital part of the house, orienting the rooms and porches to truly claim the dramatic view, balancing common and private spaces, creating a smooth flow through the rooms, all without overwhelming the good basic proportions of the original building with the new work.

Of course, it is too much to say that this handful of ideas was *all* that mattered. There are so many issues at stake in home design, including heating, cooling, shedding water, and getting the building to stand up properly. Nevertheless, it did seem that a few patterns were the indispensable keys to the architectural success of the house. Without them, the house might be safe and dry, but it might also have been awkward, graceless, and out of tune with those qualities that, in elemental human terms, make it work—make it a place that looks intuitively right, a place that, above all, feels good to be in.

The house already possessed some of these patterns. There was a sweet veranda on the southwest side; the old roof had a simple hipped form with a real emotional punch; and there was an honesty in the brown shingle look of the place, which seemed perfectly at home on its northern California site. In such cases, the important thing is to let be—to revitalize and renovate but, finally, to work

An old brown-shingled, wood-frame convent is transformed into a single-family home. A few archetypal patterns make all the difference. The eyebrow dormer, reflecting the curve of the surrounding hills (Parts in Proportion), lets natural light into the dark interior (Capturing Light), helps establish an entrance transition (The Flow through Rooms), and makes the roof a habitable place (Sheltering Roof).

with and amplify the great features of the building. In other respects, however, the house was devoid of patterns we thought essential—the interiors were far too dark; where south light existed, it was harsh and glary; and the circulation through the house was gloomy and in some places rather tortuous. The basic design problem, then, was to work with the successful old patterns, harmonizing them with new forms and features to make the house a wedding of old and new—to make it, in short, an old/new house.

The convent house was literally an old house made new. But we can usefully apply these concepts to new construction as well. Our basic patterns are not original ideas; they spring from human nature and have been part of residential architecture for centuries. Working with the patterns leads to buildings that have the qualities of older houses, but older houses made new, made into places that capture the timeless essence of home.

Lengthening the small existing veranda transformed it into one of the key spaces of the house, a place between inside and out.

Buildings should be arranged to increase exposure to the site's best features, minimize unwanted intrusions, and show respect for neighboring homes.

INHABITING THE SITE

This house flows into its site— spanning a creek, nestling in between trees—so that while living in the house the owners truly inhabit the site.

UNLESS YOU'RE FORTUNATE ENOUGH TO LIVE on a houseboat or in a motor home, your house will be anchored to a piece of land. Like a tree grabbing a roothold in the slope, reaching down for water and minerals and arching up toward the available sunlight, a house must begin and grow from its site. When the design of a house has grown out of the uniqueness of its site, it will seem as natural and as integral a part of the whole as trees are a part of the forest. When the house becomes a part of the land, the site can be fully inhabited.

BELONGING TO THE SITE

Site planning is the first step in the process of creating a home. Deciding where the main pieces of the building, the paths and roads, and the gardens go are decisions that affect every choice that follows. They are a major factor in shaping the final form of the house. When this is done well, the rest of the design flows and develops smoothly, but when there are unresolved problems in the site plan, they can never be fully overcome in the later design.

If the form of the house doesn't begin by responding to the site,

A special feature of the site that's easily seen from the house provides a great opportunity for marrying the house to the land.

This house in northern California is placed just close enough to the oak trees that they become a part of daily living.

house and site may well end up in conflict with each other. The house may be founded on unstable soil or it may be built on the very spot that was the most beautiful and useful space on the site, preventing you from ever enjoying it again. The sun may not reach the building in the winter, but beat down on it in the summer. The windows of the building may not capture the best views but instead gaze awkwardly into the neighbors' house. In the worst case, the house may end up feeling like it simply doesn't belong on the site.

But while there are dangers, there are also great opportunities in shaping a site plan. If some special feature of the site—a rock outcropping, a graceful tree, or a dramatic view—can easily be seen from within the house, the residents will be able to sense and appreciate their place in nature on a daily basis. If the buildings help shape a sheltered, south-facing outdoor space, the residents will be encouraged to step out into the warmth of the sun and to more fully experience their site. The placement of the buildings can define both an attractive public front for the site and a more private, secure back. And by responding to the placement of neighboring buildings, it is even possible to share the visual use of each other's outdoor spaces.

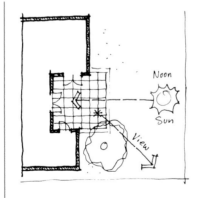

The building shapes an inviting south-facing outdoor space.

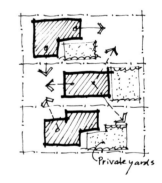

Careful placement in regard to neighboring buildings allows residents to have both private yards and to share the visual use of each other's outdoor spaces.

A HOME IN NATURE

A home needs to have a relationship with nature. In the suburbs or in the country, there's plenty of opportunity to interweave views, sun, and plantings with the buildings to achieve a comfortable balance. This can be done by extending the arms of the house out into the future garden.

On this dramatic hilltop site, sturdy rock walls grow up out of the ground, anchoring the house to nature.

Extend the buildings out into the sun and trees.

On sites with limited views, sun, or space for gardens, it's necessary to invite nature into the house, by draping the building with planted trellises and flower boxes, by creating interior window wells, or by planning courts for the penetration of light and air into the heart of the building. The house creates a habitat for nature to grow into our lives, and the plantings enrich and soften the buildings.

Some sites are dominated by nature, with dizzying views, rushing water, or bracing sea breezes. Human nature being what it is, we tend not to flee from this power but instead to build securely and then provide lookouts and pathways that allow us to venture into the very teeth of the wildness. For these sites, the buildings enrich and soften raw nature.

In all three cases, the attempt is to strongly knit the house with the site so that the people who live there will be encouraged to experience nature as deeply and confidently as possible.

Invite nature into the house.

Extending parts of the building out into the site ties the house more strongly to the land.

WORKING WITH THE PATTERN

Given a site (whether in undeveloped nature, in a suburban neighborhood, or in the city), how can the people who will live there most successfully inhabit it? Here are the essential elements for the creation of a good site plan:

◢ *Protect the heart of the site* by keeping driveways and parking toward the edges (nothing divides a lot into parts like a road) and by blocking objectionable views with buildings or plantings.

◢ *Put the main social and communal spaces on the more public part of the site* (typically the front) as a shield for the private spaces tucked into the more remote part.

◢ *Decide what part of the site is the most special;* then preserve it. Put the building close enough to enjoy it but far enough away not to destroy it.

◢ *Extend the building's wings, decks, and garden walls* out into the site to knit the house strongly to the land.

◢ *Orient the wings and rooms to the best views.*

◢ *As you locate and arrange the main elements of the building on the site,* try to make a positive contribution to the larger surroundings, to the neighborhood.

Two neighboring houses frame a shared garden, each gaining expanded views and a feeling of spaciousness.

MAKING THE MOST OF A DIFFICULT SITE

Architect Tom Bosworth was faced with the challenge of designing a house for an almost impossible site in Seattle—a site that was too small and surrounded by houses in disrepair. The lot slopes down from the front street to a back alley, where cars access garages at the bottom level, and the front doors are on the street level above.

A COURTYARD HOUSE *Like a Roman courtyard house, this home extends out to the edges of the site, leaving space for sun, air, and landscaping in the center.*

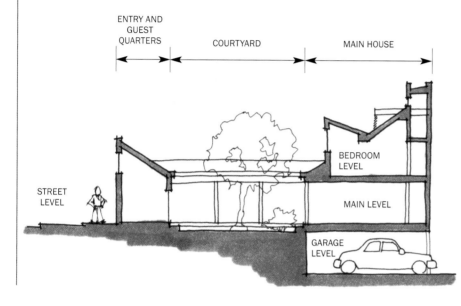

ENTRY AND
GUEST
QUARTERS | COURTYARD | MAIN HOUSE

BEDROOM
LEVEL

STREET
LEVEL

MAIN LEVEL

GARAGE
LEVEL

This house controls its site by establishing the private outdoor space behind a solid, almost blank wall on the street.

Working together, the owners and architect hit on the model of an inward-turning Roman courtyard house. They felt that only by first establishing a solid sense of security could they establish real control and habitability of their site. The solution was to build out on all sides as far as possible with relatively blank walls and thereby capture a completely interior courtyard open to the sky.

From the street, the house is austere, even a little forbidding, but it does a good job of claiming its site, defining its edges and presenting a strong fencelike appearance to the street. The floor plan (at right) reveals that the front door doesn't open to the house proper but to a covered outdoor portico running along the edge of the courtyard, passing a small guest unit on the street side, and leading back to the front door of the main house. The double stairs lead up to two bedrooms over the kitchen and dining/living commons and down to the garage below.

The courtyard becomes the entire site of the house, serving as the airy, open sunlit space for the guest suite and the main house. And

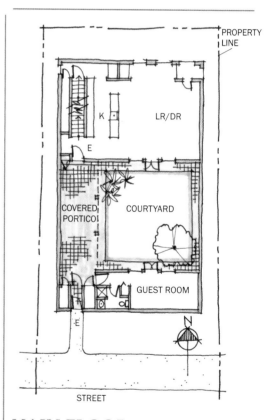

PROPERTY
LINE

K | LR/DR

E

COVERED
PORTICO | COURTYARD

GUEST ROOM

E

N

STREET

MAIN FLOOR *The entry on the street level leads to an interior courtyard, open to the sky, bounded by the guest room on the south, the main commons on the north, and a covered portico connecting them.*

From the entry on the street, a covered portico along the edge of the interior courtyard leads toward the door to the main living area of the house.

the portico doubles as a covered and shaded seating area. This atrium house solution is as effective today as it was in ancient Rome in creating a secure and inviting relationship between home and nature. It is explored further in the pattern CAPTURING LIGHT.

THE CHALLENGE OF SLOPING SITES

Houses should encourage use and appreciation of the outdoor surroundings. This requires the building to extend out into the site. Specifically, rooms should have windows and doors that open onto an adjacent outdoor space; there should be some protection over the door so it can remain open even during a brief shower; and decks and garden walls should give support and draw the residents outdoors. This is especially challenging on steeply sloping lots, because there are no existing flat areas to move out into naturally. These places have to be created, by a combination of decks and terraces.

AN UPSLOPE SITE

After their home was destroyed in the Oakland/Berkeley Hills firestorm of 1991, the Distlers asked us to help them design a new house for their upslope lot. Amazingly, much of the original terraced garden survived the fire, and linking the old garden to the new home was very important to the owners. The basic problem was finding a way to arrange the various indoor living levels so that they would have access to the existing outdoor spaces.

By keeping the house to the northeast side of the lot, and by dividing the building into a number of gradually ascending levels, we were able to provide southwest-facing outdoor areas for each floor of the house as it stepped up the slope. The var-

A FOUR-LEVEL SITE *This house is tied to its uphill site by a series of terraces, each connected to a different level of the house and to each other.*

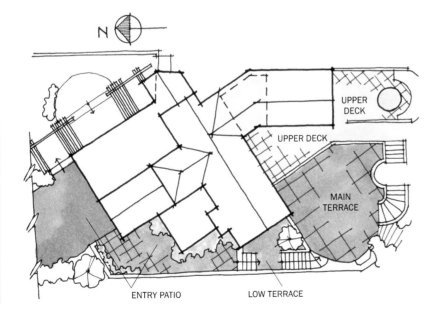

Each room opens out onto a sunny deck or terrace, inviting full use of the site.

CLIMBING THE SITE *The house climbs the hill, with each interior space connecting to an adjacent outdoor space.*

- UPPER DECK

- MAIN TERRACE

- LOW TERRACE
- ENTRY PATIO

ON THE LEVEL *The main level of the house begins (on the right) as a sheltered northern deck connected to the ground, moves to the major interior living spaces, and finally emerges as a south-facing deck that offers sun and view.*

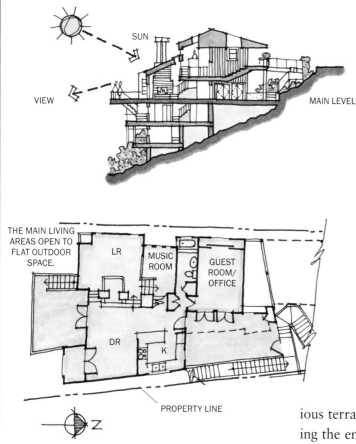

The sheltered northern deck off the commons connects the house strongly with its site. The cantilevered landing above leads to the front door.

ious terraces were then linked to each other by outdoor stairs. Locating the entry on the northeast side of the house helped preserve the privacy of all these outdoor areas.

A DOWNSLOPE SITE

Downslope lots present a similar site challenge of creating a series of flat levels for outdoor living. In our design for another residence in the Oakland-Berkeley Hills, the main level is well aboveground, but because it is extended back to meet the slope, it reconnects to the earth. And in the opposite direction, the main level reaches out to create a spectacular viewing deck, high above the ground, in full south sun. The result is that all the rooms on the main level—kitchen, dining room, living room, and office—are closely connected to flat outdoor spaces. Later in this chapter, we will see two other houses (one in the Pacific Northwest and one in New England) that extend themselves out into their flatter landscapes.

PUBLIC FRONTS, PRIVATE BACKS

It's almost always a good idea to put the main social and communal spaces on the more public portion of the site (typically the front) and to tuck the private spaces into the more remote portion out in back. In this way, the public parts of the building shield the more private parts from unwanted exposure to visitors. A particularly effective example of this is offered by a house in West Seattle designed by Jill Sousa for the Johnson Partnership.

Sousa coaxed a beautifully livable plan out of a 60-ft.-wide by 150-ft.-deep upslope lot by providing two one-car garages (instead of the typical two-car garage) and placing them perpendicular to each other at the bottom end of the lot. The space between is just wide enough to form a gateway to the upper portion of the site beyond. The main living and work spaces are located on this upper level, over the two garages, a level removed from the public street.

An office/shop is built over the front garage and the main house over the other garage, creating the long south-facing main outdoor space between them, which is reached by a flight of outdoor steps. The office/shop not only helps enclose and define the upper garden but also protects it from the public street and sidewalk. The private rooms are a story above the commons and look down into the yard from the security of a higher level.

The upper yard is shaped by the two buildings, given greater privacy by being a level higher than the street, and correctly oriented to the sun.

The resulting upper yard is a sunny, south-facing outdoor space, which is much appreciated in the cool northwest climate. By placing the house to the north side of the site rather than centering it in the conventional way, Sousa turned a potentially useless side yard into the central outdoor area.

Next, we'll look at a site with dramatic natural features, along with some real problems. The way it was developed illustrates all the elements of this pattern presented so far, along with a new concept—the need to preserve the best parts of the site.

The driveway and garages are on the lower street-level forecourt, while the main sunny yard is a level above, accessed by gracefully curving outdoor stairs.

A PROTECTED SITE

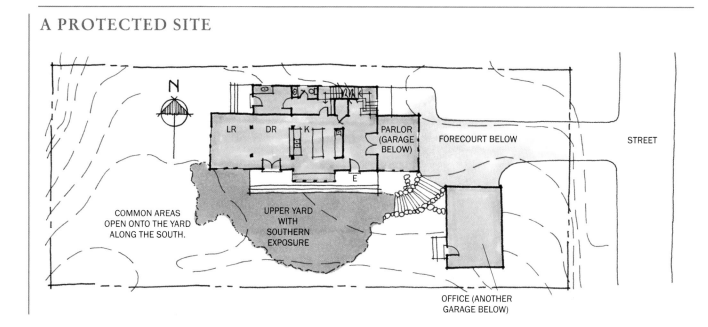

Reaching Out into the Site

SOME SITES COMMUNICATE THEIR DEMANDS very clearly. When architect Henry Klein visited the lakeside site in Washington State that Peter Johanson selected for his new home, he faced a wealth of opportunities. Located on a quiet country road, the site is defined along two sides by the edge of a lake. Generous in size and blessed with excellent exposure to the south, the site slopes gently down to a richly varied shoreline. There's a small cove that supports a population of otters, and the rich surrounding forest of cedar and fir includes a meandering seasonal stream that flows down through the middle of the site toward the lake. With all this bounty come challenges: The lake rises

The house is knitted into the site as naturally as a living thing. In partnership with the closest trees, the building forms semi-enclosed outdoor rooms that can be enjoyed by sitting on steps or an old fallen tree or can be explored by hopping across the creek on stepping-stones.

*Decide what part of the site is the most special;
then preserve it. Put the building close enough to
enjoy it but far away enough not to destroy it.*

3 ft. in the winter, setback requirements limited the use of some parts of the land, and views of neighboring houses required screening.

The owner's demands were simple. He requested a single-story building to accommodate his elderly mother, and he hoped for a design that would hide and protect the views of the lake. Given this extraordinary site, Klein conceived of a house that would sit lightly above the land, safe from the winter rains. Necessity and desire conspired to help produce a novel approach to the site design: The setbacks from the property lines and from the seasonally changing lake shore, combined with the owner's insistence on a one-story accessible house, suggested a plan that used both sides of the stream. The house would be composed of three separate buildings: the garage, which forms a gateway; a quiet bedroom building; and a noisier commons building. The buildings are separated so that each can sit in a unique place on the site, but they are linked by an enclosed bridge that spans the stream and extends into a boardwalk, reaching out toward the water.

The delicacy and transparency of the enclosed bridge are made possible by the diagonal steel rods in the bridge walls, which enable the structure to span the entire streambed.

THE APPROACH TO THE HOUSE

Entry to the site is by car, along a 100-ft.-long gravel driveway to the garage. Although the driveway is a little long (about a third of the site's depth), it offers a number of advantages:

- It provides a gently turning entry transition, away from the road, through some sizable trees, before coming to a crunchy stop at the garage doors.

- It makes it possible to place the garage at a comfortable distance from the main house across the stream.

- It brings us deep enough into the site that we get a glimpse of the excitement to come, but just a hint.

Once you're out of the car, a brick path first invites a pause and a look at the stream flowing through the site. The next thing you notice is the house ahead, stretched across, and partly shielding, a first glimpse of the lake beyond. Then a wooden ramp comes into view, which leads the eye to the front door. The house is the gateway to the rest of the site.

The building's point foundations allow plants, animals, and the seasonally rising lake to pass freely under the house.

At the front of the garage, the house and its front door come into view, but the buildings shield a full view of the lake beyond. The entire building complex is the gateway to the larger view beyond.

The enclosed bridge over the stream (facing page) leads to the commons building.

The site plan allows the stream to unify the site: Crossing the stream from within the house becomes a memorable experience.

A HEALTHY SITE PLAN

The stream could have been thought of as a site divider, with the entire house built between it and the road. A more timid approach might then have placed the building nearer the road and left the beauty of the stream and its environs intact, to be a feature distant and apart from the house. Or an excessively aggressive approach might have dominated the site, perhaps diverting the stream to make room for a larger house site enfronting the lake.

The chosen plan brings the residents in touch with the whole site, placing them in different and distinct areas of the site as they carry out their daily routines; so that by simply using the house, they are brought into contact with the outdoors. The house lets the site flow around, through, and under it. This ongoing awareness of the whole site helps establish a mutual benefit—the site will continue to nourish the residents, and they in turn will continue to care for and maintain the site.

A HOUSE ON LAKE AND STREAM

Buildings and pathways extend out to the site to bring the residents into intimate contact with all aspects of their natural surroundings. The site flows into (and under) the dwelling itself.

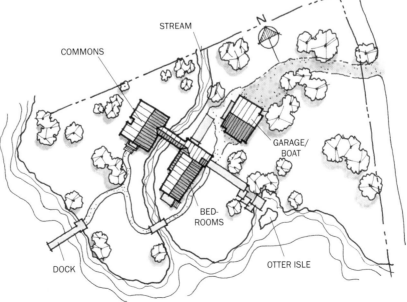

DON'T BUILD
ON THE BEST SPOT

One of the most common mistakes in site planning is to place the building on the best spot on the site. It might be a sunny clearing that invites you to stop and enjoy the warmth or a tree that offers cooling shade, a possible place for a picnic, and a great view below. Instead of putting the building on the picnic spot, pull it back a bit to form a backdrop (and a windbreak) for generations of future picnickers.

Building a house and shaping the spaces that surround it is a purposeful manipulation of the natural world, an active attempt to inhabit the land and make it our own. To inhabit is to enter into a more permanent relationship with a place. We try not to damage what the site offers willingly, as we make bold, permanent modifications to shape it to our desires. Just as the flora and fauna exploit and help shape the landscape, we build paths and roads and dig sound foundations, permanently altering the site as we stake our claim on it.

But we mustn't destroy the features that brought us to the site in the first place. Normally this means that on sloping sites, any flat portion should be preserved for outdoor activities, and the house should be built on the adjacent slope, with the floor level connected to the flat area.

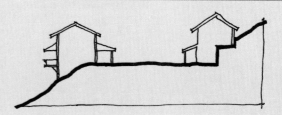

Preserve any flat portions of sloping sites for outdoor activities.

It's common knowledge that you must build outside the drip line of a treasured tree to ensure its survival. In the same way, you should back away from any interesting site feature the distance of a room to preserve its capacity to help form an outdoor room and to be visible from inside the house.

When you visit the site, note where you usually pause and sit for a while. That spot is probably a good place to point the building toward—or even to embrace on a couple of sides with building wings.

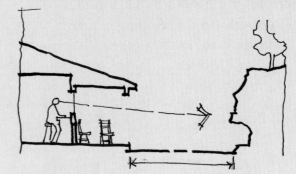

Back away from any interesting site feature at least the distance of a room.

STEPPING LIGHTLY ON THE SITE

Instead of digging deeply into the earth to establish massive foundations, the architect designed the building so that it appears to float above the stream and land. The structure respectfully treats the lake shore and forest floor as features that can be most effectively enjoyed by stepping gently across them, allowing fish, animals, and plants to pass or grow unimpeded below. This feature, of course, is imperative

when the lake does indeed rise during winter, sometimes flowing completely under the structures. The buildings touch the ground periodically on widely separated pressure-treated wooden posts, each diagonally braced back up to the building for stiffness (see the photo on p. 35).

Roads and paths on the ground are constructed of gravel (for cars) and bark (for paths under trees) to preserve the permeability and life below in the soil. The point-support type of foundation used in this house is appropriate for a fragile forest floor and shoreline, whereas a rockier site would dictate a more spread out, massive foundation. Inhabiting the Site means establishing a sustainable structure that is finely tuned to the particulars of the site.

ALIGNING TO THE VIEWS

Each of the three major buildings, the walkway bridge, and the various ramps are aligned with natural features beyond, a subtle but powerful way of linking the structures to the site. The bedroom and the commons each line up with the best view of the lake beyond, to the southwest. This southwest orientation guarantees that the outdoor space formed by these two buildings and their connecting bridge gets good direct sunlight during the day—and the interior of the bridge gets free heating. The outdoor space is also less windy because of the protection provided by the surrounding buildings.

SITED FOR VIEWS *The commons building is separated from the rest of the house and aligned with the major view. The quieter bedrooms orient to the secondary view, a cove where wildlife gathers, reached by the long walkway to the east.*

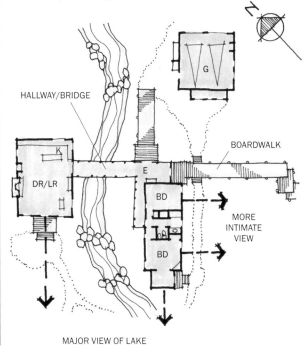

HALLWAY/BRIDGE

BOARDWALK

MORE INTIMATE VIEW

MAJOR VIEW OF LAKE

The landscaping is as restrained as the simple forms of the architecture.

The interiors are simple and Shaker-like, allowing the emphasis to be on the surrounding site and its variety and detail.

The line of the bridge extends out beyond the house along a raised wooden boardwalk toward a special feature of the shore, a small cove guarded by an islet and surrounded by rocks—a spot that invites more intimate, quiet, and secret exploration of the water and shore. The architect placed the quieter bedroom wing closer to this natural feature than the commons wing to guarantee that the wildlife would remain on the site, available for silent observation from deck chairs set up on the boardwalk.

UNDERSTATED BUILDINGS LET THE SITE SPEAK

The simplicity of the architecture complements the strong presence of the site. The various parts of the buildings are modest in scale and simple in shape; nothing overpowers or outshines the site. Each of the

three main elements has a rectangular, gabled house form, with modifying gestures of porch additions and roof overhangs. The materials are limited to cedar-shingled walls and unpainted corrugated zinc-aluminum metal roofs. Window and door trim is kept in natural wood. All of these are cabinlike choices that age and weather to fit perfectly into their wooded setting.

Landscape architect Richard Haag used a similarly restrained touch, adding just a few, carefully placed elements. Deciduous aspen trees, which are tolerant of periodic flooding, were planted at the foot of the main entry ramp and on the west side of the buildings, where they provide partial shade from low summer afternoon sun.

Finally, the interior spaces are kept similarly simple and pure so they don't detract from the richness of the trees, sky, and water. They are executed with the same economy and directness of purpose that characterize the entire design. Everywhere you look, there's a fresh, invigorating sense of "just what is needed, nothing more." Because the basic needs of shelter and security are provided so simply and directly, we're invited to experience the site in just the same way.

Viewed from the dock, the house is composed of simple geometric forms that call to mind rural structures and offer a foil to the richness of the surrounding natural organic forms.

New Buildings in a Historic Neighborhood

Let's turn now from the primeval Northwest forests to a historic Massachusetts neighborhood, with a house that illustrates the same site-planning principles we've already discussed but, in addition, makes a positive contribution to the surrounding neighborhood. It's also an example that involves historical precedent—the gradual development of a site over 180 years.

The owners wanted to expand and convert a historic building, known originally as the Captain Jethro Ripley house, into a year-round home, with a new garage, kitchen, dining, and master bedroom wing and with better use of the garden. But they were equally committed to preservation of the original 1820 portion of the house and to a remodel that would enhance and reinforce the historic value of the house and the larger neighborhood. The owners chose architects Donald Corner and Jenny Young to help with a design that would be a response not only to the site and its natural conditions of sun, space, and views but also to the history of the building and its neighborhood.

The strong historical context of the location demanded that the addition be executed within the same scale and language of the neighborhood—with similarly sized building blocks, similarly sloped roofs, and similar colors and detailing.

A BOLD REMODEL PRESERVES THE HISTORIC FEELING

The evolution of the site over the years, shown on p. 45, provides background for the design that was eventually adopted. Captain Ripley bought the original house from an outlying farmer and moved the building to its present city-center site in 1820, locating it right on the corner of Cooke Street, facing School Street. A few years later,

Even from inside the house, there's a constant reminder of the surrounding historic neighborhood.

The dining table sits in a bay of windows, which allows real appreciation of the site's warm southern light and a filtered view of the neighborhood beyond.

IMPROVING
THE NEIGHBORHOOD

Almost every potential building site is subject to city or county zoning, which limits the house's location on the property, height, minimum number of parking spaces, and maximum number of kitchens. Some communities have even more detailed Covenants, Codes, and Restrictions (CC&Rs), which dictate minimum sizes, exterior materials, and colors. The negative way to look at these restrictions is that they legislate conformity. A more positive view is that they point toward opportunities for individual designs to improve, fit into, and enrich the surrounding fabric of the neighborhood.

Beyond zoning and CC&Rs, here are some specific ways that site planning can potentially improve the neighborhood:

■ Preserve your neighbors' access to winter sun by positioning your house and landscaping low on their south side. (Blocking their late summer afternoon sun from the west, on the other hand, might actually help them avoid overheating.)

■ Locate your building and windows to permit views into neighbors' public yards, getting double "viewing mileage" from those spaces. Other windows can profitably face onto a neighbor's blank wall, especially if those walls are covered with attractive siding or plantings.

■ Avoid windows that look directly into neighbors' windows or down into their private outdoor spaces. This will create discomfort for both of you.

■ Share the most important views. The more houses that benefit, the healthier the whole neighborhood. In hilly neighborhoods, this usually means limiting the height of trees to the heights of the buildings.

■ Try to use some of the predominant stylistic elements of the neighboring homes, adjusting them to your situation and taste.

Ripley added a kitchen wing on the north, using lumber his ship had carried in from Maine. Still later, a Victorian porch was added along the kitchen wing facing the garden, and several outbuildings were added to the property over the years. Finally, in 1974 a small, modern kitchen shed was added to the end of the old addition.

Working with their architects, the owners came up with a novel overall plan. They decided to locate all their private living needs in a new addition and to use the original house as guest quarters and as

The Cooke Street side of the house is unified by the repetition of the original building's shapes, materials, and window details in the addition. The new entrance is set between the original building on the right and the addition to the left.

the common living room. In addition to adding the new structures, the architects proposed moving an existing outbuilding and demolishing two others to increase flexibility in site planning. Their basic concept was to place the owners' private living area in a separate two-story structure, located well north of the existing house, and to join this new structure to the old house via a new one-story connecting link. This link would then become the new entry to the entire complex. Thus the resulting building would not look like a double-size house but more like a traditional connected New England homestead, with the main house on the street, connected to the barns in the back by narrower passageways.

By offsetting the two main buildings relative to each other, the architects were able to create a new, semi-enclosed courtyard on the sunny southeast side of the resulting L-shaped building, ensuring that the new addition would get south sun (as well as a view of the nearby church spire, shown in the photo at left on p. 42). The new freestanding guest/office building helps shape the northern edge of

THE EVOLUTION OF THE SITE *The current remodel and addition take their place in a long history of site development, as the different owners expanded the buildings to accommodate their changing needs.*

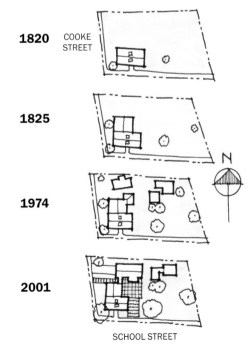

WINDOWS LINK PAST AND PRESENT *The original window dimensions are repeated throughout the new addition, sometimes in larger groups assembled from smaller window units derived from the original house.*

From the courtyard

From Cooke Street

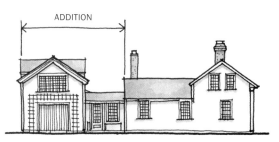

The room above the garage is fitted with unusually large windows, but their scale is kept in harmony with the rest of the house and the neighborhood.

the lot's generous yard, while the new paved courtyard links all the buildings at the heart of the yard. A new garden borders the southern end of the courtyard so it can bask in maximum sun.

From School Street, it's clear that the expansion successfully preserves the character of the original building. The new addition has virtually the same height and width as the original house, but because it's placed back from the street it takes on the appearance of a barn—or a support structure that was remodeled in later years. The white clapboard siding of the original house is changed to wood shingles on the new structure, reinforcing its more informal workaday interpretation.

The view from Cooke Street (see the photo on p. 45) is just as successful in integrating the new with the old, showing the repetition of building shape, materials, colors, and details to bind the complex into a whole. Other examples of good site planning include the use of overhead planted trellises to deemphasize the garage and the welcoming recess and low white picket fence to give emphasis to the new main entry.

TYING IT ALL TOGETHER

By repeating signature details, the architects were able to unify the original house and the addition, as well as the house and the surrounding neighborhood. A good example of this is the window treatment. Traditionally, window panes were small because of the difficulty of manufacturing larger sheets of glass. A historic home usually doesn't look right if the original small-paned windows are replaced with large-paned units. Here, the architects were careful to use the same type, size, and proportion of windows on the new addition as those on the original historic buildings, as can be seen in the drawing on the facing page. This house, like most of the homes showcased in this book, is not only a particularly strong example of Inhabiting the Site but also incorporates several other patterns as well.

A sleeping porch above the garage has very generous windows that open fully to create the feeling of both being in a protected place and having an overlook of the street life below (an example of REFUGE AND OUTLOOK). But the sash and the muntins are kept at the same scale as those of the original house to keep the house integrated with both the neighborhood and itself.

Wherever the architects needed to create a large window area, they assembled it out of several smaller window units derived from the original house. This lends an underlying unity to the variety of the windows, and in this sense, the project demonstrates PARTS IN PROPORTION.

The new entry location provides a link between the two parts of the house, connecting the garage entry to the main entry and providing access to the new courtyard space. It becomes the true pivot around which the house is now organized (THE FLOW THROUGH ROOMS) and effectively locates the public access to the house near the street, preserving most of the site for the more intimate gardens.

The addition and reconfiguration project made powerful use of the pattern CAPTURING LIGHT.

New blends seamlessly with old as the addition and existing house come together to frame a private inner courtyard.

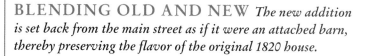

BLENDING OLD AND NEW *The new addition is set back from the main street as if it were an attached barn, thereby preserving the flavor of the original 1820 house.*

PATTERNS IN CONTEXT

The initial appeal of this historic remodel is the highly effective site plan, which keeps cars to the perimeter, puts the entry at the front, wraps around a south-facing garden, and improves the neighborhood all at the same time. But like any good house, it can also be used to illustrate several other patterns.

Capturing Light.
Large and tall windows, with low sills, flood the south-facing commons with natural light.

Sheltering Roof.
Upstairs rooms huddle under the center of the roof, pushing out dormer windows for light and additional space where needed.

Parts in Proportion.
Families of forms, such as the window-pane shape that is used in a great variety of situations throughout the building, lend an underlying unity to the house.

Composing with Materials.
Simple, dignified materials complement one another and help bind the house to its history.

Interiors maintain the historic pine floors and painted wainscoting. The upstairs bedroom is built into the roof; and by placing the closets under the lowest corner portions of the roof, the architects were able to create inviting window alcoves.

The kitchen and dining room in the new addition are placed to get south sun, and the hall from the entry to these rooms is illuminated by a whole bank of south-facing windows. From the entry hall, it's possible to get just a glimpse of the new dining alcove down at the end of the lit hall (see the photo on the facing page). And the journey is enticing because there is the promise of even more light (and view) around the dining table beyond.

The promise is fulfilled with a light-filled alcove off the main kitchen space, formed of tall double-hung windows that allow the table to be bathed in warm southern light and to feel intimately connected to the garden just outside, especially when the windows are open (see the photo on pp. 42–43). This single space in the house is a great example of the way several patterns can work together: PLACES IN BETWEEN; THE FLOW THROUGH ROOMS; PRIVATE EDGES, COMMON CORE; and CAPTURING LIGHT. In terms of this pattern, Inhabiting the Site, the alcove is a superb example of extending a portion of a building out into the site and orienting it to an important view (in this case, the garden with the neighborhood beyond).

The interiors of the addition are composed in harmony with the original historic portions of the building (COMPOSING WITH MATERIALS). The floors are wide boards of a rich brown, clear-finished knotty pine, and the wainscoting is painted gray. The neutral colors of the ceilings and walls highlight and provide counterpoint to the warm natural color of the flooring. And as in the original house, the upstairs rooms, built into and under the roof volume, have ceilings that express and echo the roof and dormer shapes (SHELTERING ROOF).

A bank of tall windows captures light for the hall-way to the dining room and for the stairs to the upper bedroom.

Transforming a Site

Site planning is the first step in transforming a piece of land into a place to live. Each of the houses featured in this chapter was based on a fortuitous decision—from turning inward to exclude unpleasant elements to extending out into the surroundings to gain further exposure to pleasant ones. Each site plan in different ways creates a gradient from public to private, while seeking ways to gain more view, sun, and air. Each capitalizes on what is unique about its site, taking care not to destroy it. And the Massachusetts house illustrates that a home site can take many years to develop fully, toward ever more unity, harmony, and integration. As the buildings have grown out into the site, they have been placed to get good light. And at the same time, the inner yard spaces have been increasingly well defined, the hierarchy of privacy has been strengthened, and the neighborhood has been enriched.

PATTERN TWO

Well-designed homes with well-proportioned, satisfying interior rooms make well-proportioned exterior rooms of the spaces around them.

CREATING ROOMS, OUTSIDE AND IN

Just as surely as it shapes the dining room and the living room beyond, this house also shapes an outdoor room, a courtyard in between.

A S YOU WALK AROUND AN EMPTY BUILDING SITE, a natural instinct is to think, "the kitchen should go here... the living room could look out in this direction...." We tend to imagine ourselves in the most important rooms of the house and think how these rooms can be oriented to fit the site. But a house, by its very presence on a site, creates outdoor rooms as well as indoor rooms. And the outdoor rooms should be as well considered and as well proportioned as the indoor rooms. In a well-designed house, there is a lively balance of indoor and outdoor rooms, and the two types of spaces form a kind of interlocking checkerboard on the site.

What makes this pattern so compelling is the fundamental idea that the critical *rooms* of a house, the rooms most used and treasured, are outside as well as in; and that, unless a house is conceived from the beginning as simultaneously shaping *both* kinds of rooms, the outdoor rooms end up as leftover spaces, without the coherence of design required to make them truly work. The indoor rooms can also suffer when a house is located and organized primarily with respect to its interiors. The indoor spaces can feel cut off from the site and can lack the in–out interplay that, regardless of climate, is so characteristic of successful homes.

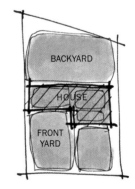

Every house creates both indoor and outdoor rooms. Even the typical suburban house—shaped without much consideration for its outdoor spaces—creates two major outdoor rooms: "the front yard" and "the backyard."

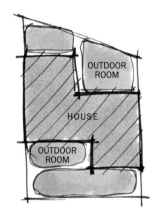

Here, the form of the house, while continuing to shape its interior rooms, more boldly shapes its exterior rooms as well.

THE ROOTS OF THE PATTERN

The roots of this pattern lie in a combination of ecological, psychological, and aesthetic factors. From an ecological point of view, rooms can be thought of as habitats. And outdoor rooms are outdoor habitats more likely to be lived in and used—and more likely, therefore, to be cared for and improved—when they are defined and tempered by the very building that is their users' primary habitat. A building that helps shape a courtyard, a greenhouse/garden room that helps shape its garden, a balcony that animates the patio below all illustrate cases in which the home, itself the primary "nest," is used to boldly delineate the outdoors immediately beside it.

In such cases, the presence of the building, if properly oriented to sun, shade, and wind, can create a microclimate and temper the outdoor room, making it all the more appealing. By comparison, outdoor areas that are largely leftover spaces, dissociated from the interiors

This courtyard is as carefully detailed as any indoor room. The low edges formed by the trellis, the low sitting wall that defines the outer edge of the court, the step-seats down from the dining room, and the two-story wing stepping down to the one-story pavilion all enhance the courtyard, helping it function as an interior room.

where people gather, tend never to become rooms of everyday use and are thus apt to be neglected.

The psychological basis for the pattern stems from the need for defensible outdoor space—space that is both enclosed enough to be securely *ours* and open enough to be part of a greater natural order. Our need for such spaces is elaborated in REFUGE AND OUTLOOK; here, it is used to help explain why an outdoor space, shaped by the home it serves, provides such pleasure. Perhaps the great secret contained by this pattern is that, just as deeply as we long for shelter, we long for sheltered gardens. And the homes that stir our souls are places that in single strokes create both. After all, the primary place of Genesis is the walled garden. Eden, architecturally, is a squarish outdoor room.

Aesthetically, the pattern tends to create rich and interesting quiltlike geometries of indoor/outdoor space. Much of the charm and intrigue of the houses examined for this pattern comes from the way the buildings make a mosaic pattern of their sites. These patterns, inherently more complex, ambiguous, and replete with order than their suburban cousins (see the drawings on p. 51 and on the facing page), are satisfying in and of themselves because they are better integrated. Houses and sites that incorporate this pattern are like paintings in which the so-called negative space is as positively and imaginatively shaped as the foreground itself.

In the photo on p. 50, an outdoor courtyard is glimpsed through a dining room; the edge of the court is defined by a living room wing and its trellis. The interior rooms are the positive captured spaces, the reason the building exists... but they are also background foils that serve to define the courtyard, with the court itself as the primary positive space. In effect, it is the interplay of closed–open–closed that makes the whole place lively, a place where each space in turn becomes a positive force in the entire ensemble.

In effect, this house contains two living rooms: the indoor one and its outdoor equivalent. A generous opening between the two helps knit them together.

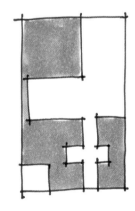

Under the impact of this pattern, a house and the space around it become an interlocking whole, each shaping the other.

A gateway becomes like a front door into an outdoor room. After the building itself, gates, fences, and trees may be used to shape outdoor rooms.

WORKING WITH THE PATTERN

Homes create rooms, indoors and out. Use this pattern to think of the major rooms your home will contain. Imagine where they will be on the site and how they will be oriented.

◢ *Let the location of the indoor rooms shape the outdoor rooms,* both the natural outdoor rooms partially created by the site and the new ones created entirely by the building.

◢ *Imagine the entire site as a sequence of roomlike places,* a checkered pattern of indoor and outdoor spaces.

◢ *The sequence of rooms will have a natural hierarchy:* Some will be large, more important, and more central; others will be supportive and transitional. Some will be for cars and people; others will be for people only. Make them all part of the pattern and make sure none is useless, leftover space.

◢ *Use wings of buildings, exterior walls, outbuildings, and breezeways* to help create the basic pattern; use plantings, low walls, terraces, and furnishings to underscore and strengthen the pattern.

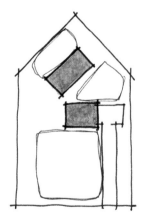

Major indoor and outdoor rooms are formed together, in interaction with the site.

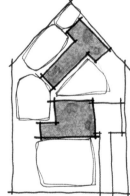

The whole site is a hierarchical sequence of indoor/outdoor rooms.

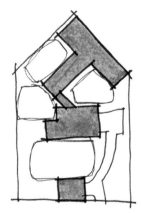

A variety of elements—walls, plantings, gateways, paths—are used to define and embellish the pattern of rooms.

A Quilt of Courts and Rooms

T HE SITE PLAN FOR THIS SMALL HOME in West Marin, California, by architect Cass Calder Smith, is a perfect example of the pattern in action. Three buildings are located on the site: a carport, an L-shaped main house, and a bedroom wing. These structures are located to orient the major indoor rooms of the house—living, dining, and so on—and to create an interconnected sequence of outdoor spaces. To clarify the way the pattern works, two colors are overlaid on the plan on p. 56: green for the major outdoor rooms and red for the indoor rooms.

The two-story portion of the house provides a strong back to the court. The flanking one-story wings give the court a comfortable scale.

Imagine the entire site as a sequence
of roomlike places, a checkered pattern
of indoor and outdoor spaces.

It's interesting to note that all the colored shapes are "positive" shapes, shapes that have an identifiable form and feel whole, not exactly squares or rectangles, but square- and rectangular-*ish*. The rectangles are never longer than 2:1, so they retain the quality of a comfortable indoor room (see PARTS IN PROPORTION). Each of the spaces is defined by elements of the building and aspects of the site. There are almost no "negative" spaces, those leftover places—often found between the major rooms—that are hard to define and to make usable. The entire site is like a quilt of interlocking, well-shaped rooms.

In terms of the pattern, the most important rooms on the site plan are the living room, the dining room/study, and the south-facing central courtyard that is in part defined by these spaces. This trio of spaces forms the central common area: the living room and dining room define and anchor the courtyard, which in turn provides an intimate outdoor room into which the living and dining rooms open.

A key reason for organizing the site this way was to use the house as a buffer against the prevailing northerly winds, creating a protected courtyard open to a view. In this climate, where days are often sunny but cool, the building tempers the microclimate of the court, making it a comfortable room.

A HIERARCHY OF ROOMS

All the other rooms on the site are developed to complement the central court arrangement. The carport, for example, is located to allow a smooth transition onto the site by car and turned so that the rear ends of the cars are not left facing the street. But this same carport, in conjunction with the north wall of the main building, also forms an outdoor arrival room for cars and pedestrians, a coherent space, reinforced by landscape, in which the cars are left behind. On its south side, the carport is used to form a small entry court, a garden to pass through as we move toward a pivoting gate that, like the true front door of the house, opens into the main courtyard.

The two-story wall and the carport together define a north-facing court, the first outdoor room, a place to arrive and to leave the car behind. The two-story "back" buffers the court on the southern side of the site from prevailing winds.

A HOUSE THAT CREATES ROOMS, OUTSIDE AND IN

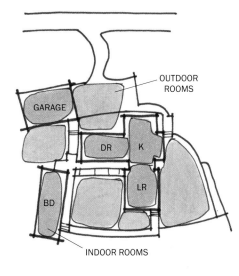

Like a front door into the house, the gate pivots into the main court. The carport has been left behind. The two trellises overlap to intensify the point of entry into the main court.

In checkerboard fashion, the carport and two-story wall create a second outdoor room: a pedestrian entry court that acts as a transitional place between the car court and the main court. The plantings, gate, and northern wall of the bedroom wing complete the definition of this outdoor room and continue the work of buffering the main court from the wind.

The main courtyard and the indoor room to its north (the dining room/study with its bedroom above) are the center of the plan. But the secondary spaces (the carport, the guest bedroom wing) are located to reinforce the pattern and to create a sequence of well-shaped rooms around the center. Like many of the farms in the area, this house uses the strategy of a building cluster to define its outdoor rooms. The house comprises three separate buildings. The living room, shaped like a one-story pavilion set off from the central two-story structure, is in effect a fourth building in the composition. The farm cluster tradition—in which yards and pens and gardens are shaped by the farmhouse, shed, and barn—is the inspiration for the site plan.

The main court is the
central outdoor room, protected from the wind and
open to the living spaces
around it. The concrete
path toward the front door
is above the court and
steps down into it, creating
informal seats at the edge
of the space. The trellis
reinforces the sense of this
space as a room, with a
low edge for circulation.

DETAILS STRENGTHEN THE PATTERN

The details of the house reinforce the overall pattern. The common rooms are each given generous openings out toward the courtyard and the views beyond. Trellised awnings create a transition that further links these rooms and the court. (This is the kind of element we will return to in PLACES IN BETWEEN.) The main paths of circulation are laid out to move along the edges of the spaces, so that the rooms are both enlivened by the comings and goings and yet left essentially intact. Landscape features—plantings and low retaining walls—are used to strengthen the shape of the rooms.

An interesting detail in this house, one that again underscores the overall pattern of spaces, is the gate that leads to the main courtyard

THE PLEASURE OF POSITIVE OUTDOOR SPACE

Positive spaces in and around buildings can be thought of as areas that have enough definition—from walls, fences, steps, trees, edges of all kinds—to be seen and experienced as coherent, nameable places. Negative spaces are those fragments of space that are often leftover around and between the positive spaces. Negative space is background space, rarely named in ordinary conversation.

Homes are often thought of as positive elements, and the space they occupy merely the negative emptiness into which they are placed. Houses designed with this attitude are like cakes on a platter, with empty space all around them. But outdoor space can be as positive as the building itself.

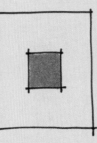

SPACE AS
NEGATIVE BACKGROUND

SPACE AS
POSITIVE PLACE

The thinking behind this pattern is that people feel more comfortable in the outdoors around their homes when that space is positive. Positive spaces tend, therefore, to be used more than negative ones and so are more likely to be developed and improved. Negative outdoor space tends to be unused and avoided.

Rotating on the pivot point established by the red gate, the bedroom wing swings out, about 10 degrees beyond the expected 90-degree corner, giving the outdoor room an expansive feeling toward the south. This rotation also serves to give an informal quality to the space, in the tradition of the odd, not-quite-right-angled corners found in vernacular courtyard buildings.

(see the top photo on p. 57). The gate functions almost like a front door, but a door that is properly scaled to the large courtyard. Passing along the west edge of the main building, through the entry garden, you arrive at the gate, which seems almost ceremonial in the way it pivots, opening into the corner of the courtyard. The gate is glazed, but the panes are translucent, not clear, except for one at eye level that provides a glimpse into and through the room beyond. The pivot point of the gate defines the corner off which the bedroom wing itself pivots, a detail that subtly underscores the roomlike shape of the main court.

The living room is a pavilion, slightly detached from the main building.

A PAVILION WITHIN THE COURT

A close look at the design of the living room reveals a subtle variation in the way the architect is working with the pattern. With its low, gently curving roof, the room is like a pavilion set apart from the rest of the building. This effect is amplified by the entry foyer, the steps down into the room, and the way the fireplace is situated with its back to the rest of the house. The broad sliding-glass doors, which open on three sides, allow the room itself to become an "outdoor room." Looking back at the site plan on p. 56, we note that the main courtyard can be seen as part of a larger swath of outdoor space with the living room pavilion at its center. The living room is *both* a background shape that helps define the foreground of the court *and* a "positive" foreground all its own, set in the middle of a field of open "negative" space.

With its subtle design and ingenious site plan, this home provides a powerful introduction to Creating Rooms, Outside and In and illustrates how even a small home can embody the pattern in rich and complex ways. Next we'll look at a house on a larger site by the same architect, which presents a slightly more intricate example.

Open on three sides, the room gives definition to the courtyard but is also like an outdoor room itself, a variation on an old-fashioned screened porch.

With its doors open, the living room becomes a shady outdoor room between the main courtyard and the terrace to the east.

Indoors and Outdoors Form a Loose Weave

LIKE THE WEST MARIN HOUSE just featured, this residence in Napa Valley, California, is modest in scale—three bedrooms, with common spaces that are open to one another. But while the first house was tightly organized around its central court, this house, on a larger site, has a more relaxed, ranch-house-type order, and it creates its outdoor rooms with a series of simple, understated gestures.

The house takes its initial cue from the mature oak grove on the site. The oaks create majestic outdoor rooms, which the architect wisely chose not to try to improve on. The site plan brackets one part of the grove with parking and the other with the north side of the main building, inviting the owners and their guests to get out of their cars and walk through these magnificent "rooms." According to

SITE PLAN *The architectural elements of the site plan are parking, main building, and bedroom wing. These elements are arranged to produce a sequence of three outdoor rooms: (1) oak grove, (2) entry porch/breezeway, and (3) a large, protected south-facing outdoor room.*

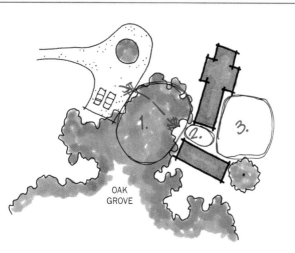

OAK GROVE

The two-story section with its south-facing gable interrupts the low, horizontal lines of the one-story common room and creates an implied edge to the outdoor room.

The whole site plan originates from the porch/breezeway. It unites the south and north sides of the site and the two wings of the building. As you arrive from the north, the space is like a threshold to the larger outdoor rooms beyond.

From the edge of the grove, the process of arrival begins with a path through the natural outdoor rooms created by the oaks. In contrast to the grove, the small, roofed entry porch offers itself as an intimate space, signifying arrival.

architect Cass Calder Smith, it was his walks through and around the oaks that inspired the location of the house and entrance. In contrast to the scale of the oaks, the breezeway/entry is an intimate space, formed by a roofed gap in the building.

This appealing space, almost perfectly square, is at once a front porch, a connecting breezeway, and, in the hot Napa Valley summers, a shady retreat from the large outdoor room to the south. But it is a gateway as well—a threshold to the open outdoor room beyond.

Use wings of buildings, exterior walls, outbuildings, and breezeways to help create the basic pattern.

CAPTURING OUTDOOR ROOMS

The large open space to the south offers an interesting case of how you can create a variety of outdoor rooms with even a relatively small amount of building. The bedroom wing to the west and the living room wing to the east are rectangles turned 90 degrees to the main common room formed by the breezeway/entry-kitchen-dining space. This allows the wings to help define a court. At the living room end, adding a small second-floor room (the third bedroom) and turning the ridgeline creates a gable end toward the open space, in contrast to the lower eave/ridgeline that fronts the space over the central section of the building.

This simple gesture—the living room extends only a few feet proud of the central part of the building—"captures" a large outdoor room, a room that includes the pool and is in scale a worthy companion to

A SMALL HOME CAPTURES A LARGE OUTDOOR ROOM

A rectangle turned to form a right angle with the main rectangular common rooms, the bedroom wing helps define the outdoor space to the south. This space is marked at its other end by the simple gesture of letting the living room bump out and form a secondary rectangle across the kitchen-dining space. This two-story element, with its ridge turned to emphasize the end of the building complex, creates the edge of the large outdoor room.

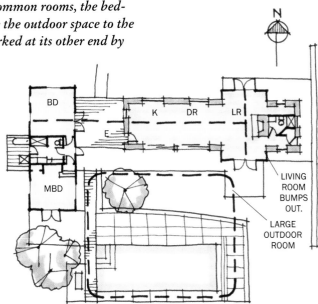

BD

K   DR   LR

E

MBD

N

LIVING ROOM BUMPS OUT.

LARGE OUTDOOR ROOM

While the Napa Valley house is a classic example of Creating Rooms, Outside and In, it serves equally well as an example of three other patterns.

Inhabiting the Site. The site plan is organized to keep the car at bay and to let its users comfortably inhabit the natural site. Building wings and walks are organized to bring residents into daily contact with the nature of the place.

Sheltering Roof. Much of the interior and exterior character of the house comes from its roof, a simple but refined composition of gables and sheds. Like the Aldermarsh residence, described on p. 85, an open roof is used to mark the point of arrival and to form an appealing outdoor space right in the middle of the house. The roof is "inhabited" in a couple of ways: A loft is built into the attic above the children's bedroom, and a study is carved into the roof above the living room.

Places in Between. The two arbors, the breezeway, and the colonnade form a necklace of places in between along the southern edge of the building.

The house is organized to delineate one large outdoor room to the south, a room that is the open-to-the-sky counterpart of the great oak-tangled room to the north. The house itself sits modestly in between. This space is far less defined than the courtyard in the West Marin house, but building and landscape work together to give it the feel of a positive outdoor space.

The vine-covered trellis off the master bedroom is a small private outdoor room, a variation of Private Edges, Common Core. The front entry porch at the end of the walk also acts like an interior alcove off the larger outdoor room.

the space created by the oaks. The outdoor room includes a number of smaller spaces, comparable to the way an interior great room can be ringed with smaller spaces, lower edges, alcoves, and inglenooks. First, there are two arbors at the opposite crossing wings. These "alcoves" both punctuate the wings, extending them into the landscape, and create small private outdoor rooms, places that are off the great court but not in it. In a similar way, the deep shady overhang along the central section—which seems to leak out from the breezeway—creates a band of space, like the lower edges that make high-ceilinged spaces feel so comfortable.

The architect uses material changes deftly and simply to reinforce the pattern of spaces. The change in color and material on the exterior from the green-painted vertical siding on the wings to the earth-toned rammed-earth walls at the center elegantly emphasizes the thrust of the wings and seems to expand their capacity to define the space to the east. This way of using materials to embody the conceptual patterns of a house is discussed in detail in COMPOSING WITH MATERIALS, but it is so well executed in this project that we can't help but mention it here.

THE INDOOR ROOM

We have been concentrating on the outdoor rooms created by the site plan, but the room at the heart of the plan is, naturally enough, indoors: the long, thick-walled kitchen-dining-living space anchored by a fireplace at one end and the breezeway at the other. This space, which is open to the courtyard and the sheltering eaves, is a compressed indoor version of the expansive outdoor room to its south.

One of the smaller and more detailed ways that this house creates rooms, outside and in, can be seen on the extreme west end of the complex, where the bedroom wing nestles into one edge of the oak grove. This meeting of building and grove alone creates a private, mysterious space, but again the architect seizes the opportunity and

The trellis off the two-story gable wall extends the living room directly out into the outdoor room. The trellis provides filtered light for the living room itself (see Capturing Light) and for the terrace—an example of the way a building can work to temper the outdoor spaces immediately beside it and make it more likely that people will use them.

The large interior room at the center of the house (and of the site plan) is the indoor equivalent of the large outdoor room on the right that it opens toward.

A small private outdoor room on the west side of the bedroom wing extends the bathroom into the oak grove. The building and site come together to create a magical outdoor Place in Between.

makes something special. Off the main bath, and again with the simplest of means, he has fashioned a tiny outdoor room for summer bathing under the trees.

A PATTERN FOR ALL CLIMATES

The two homes we've featured for this pattern are both located in the relatively mild northern California climate. The pattern, however, translates to any region and any climate. Vernacular versions of the pattern can be found in northern European and Japanese farmhouses, in Mediterranean hill towns, and in courtyard houses in desert climates. Let's look at a group of houses that illustrate some of this range.

SOUTH TEXAS COURTYARDS

Finding inspiration in the ranch houses of the southwest, Lake/Flato Architects, of San Antonio, have explored this pattern in a series of extraordinary courtyard homes for Texas sites. Two of them are illustrated here. The first, on a coastal plain in south Texas, is almost monastic, with individual rooms strung like beads around a central courtyard. The rooms are each given the shape they require. Then, linked to one another with bathrooms, breezeways, and other service spaces, they are arranged to create two magnificent outdoor rooms: the long rectangular court, which contains a pool, and the more nearly square court shaped around a single mature oak, its canopy providing a shade-dappled roof.

Like the Napa Valley home by Cass Calder Smith, the house is sited on the edge of an oak grove and uses the natural outdoor rooms formed by the oaks. The oak court, which invites us into its center to sit under the tree, creates an appealing contrast to the central court,

The extended eaves and supporting columns create a Place in Between that helps weave together the two great rooms—indoor and outdoor.

The cloisterlike walk that bounds the court and links the rooms combines traditions of European classicism with the Mexican hacienda.

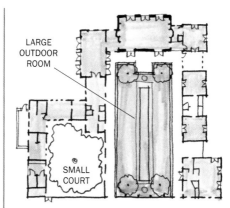

LARGE OUTDOOR ROOM

SMALL COURT

The interior rooms are individual pavilions linked to form a large rectangular outdoor room. A smaller square space is shaped around a single large oak.

which invites us to walk around the pool and garden and to sit along its edge.

The second Lake/Flato house, whose ranch-style roots are more recognizable, uses a deep, shady arcade to form the two sides of a court that contains a cluster of mesquite trees. The arcade leans against the rooms of the house and then opens up to become a breeze-way as it marches around the great outdoor room. About 12 ft. wide, the arcade is deep enough to contain a sequence of outdoor rooms within it—sitting area, dining area, even a sleeping porch.

*Let the location of the indoor rooms shape
the outdoor rooms, both the natural outdoor
rooms partially created by the site and new
ones created entirely by the building.*

Built around a grove of mesquite trees, the outdoor room is spacious and informal. The intimate outdoor spaces are contained in the arcade itself. The white brick columns form a striking contrast to the dark twisted trunks of the mesquites, enhancing the visual pleasure of each.

NORTHWEST OUTDOOR ROOMS
CARVED OUT OF CORNERS

The two Lake/Flato houses are courtyard designs that contain an outdoor space and wrap the house around it. But homes can take an opposite tack; they can be located at the center of their site and be surrounded by a sequence of outdoor rooms. The residence in Washington State (shown on p. 73) by architects Larry Johnson and Jill Sousa is a simple two-story gable form, surrounded by a lower, one-story roof. The four corners of the house are carved away to become four outdoor rooms, each with a different function in response to the adjacent interior spaces. The southeast corner, near the entry, is an entry porch; the southwest corner, off the dining room, is a communal outdoor room; the northwest corner serves the bedroom; and the northeast corner is a covered work space off the utility room. Each of the four outdoor spaces implies a larger outdoor realm, and each room can be understood as an alcove off this outer realm. This is a case of a relatively small home that is able to create a large array of positive outdoor rooms around it.

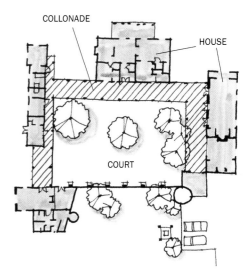

The rooms of the house spread out and alternate with walls and colonnade to surround the court and give it an almost public scale, like buildings around an old town square.

GHOST ROOMS

An interesting version of this pattern was created by architect Henry Klein in a house he designed on a narrow lot on Puget Sound. (Klein is also the architect of the Johanson house described in Inhabiting the Site.) In this project, he created a sequence of inside and outside rooms using garage, guest cabin, garden, and main house.

At the rear, the floor plan of the house is arranged to form a terrace with three more positive outdoor spaces, two serving the commons of the house and one off the master bedroom. What is entirely surprising is the series of low, odd-angled retaining walls that march down the land away from the house. These walls create flat, terraced places for gardening. Like the

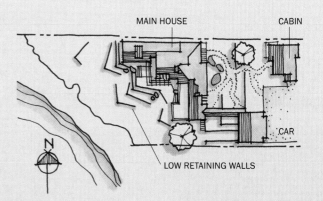

The site plan sets up an interplay of major indoor and outdoor rooms as it moves from garage through courtyard to house and decks.

foundations of an old building, these retained corners—all at perfect sitting height—create the impression of ghost rooms stepping down the slope.

A sequence of rooms culminates in the rear yard, with an unexpected cascade of low retaining/sitting walls. The walls look like old foundations and suggest the presence of ancient rooms stepping down the site.

The four outdoor rooms, each defined by two walls and a post, open the house to the landscape in a powerful way. Each corner of the house forms a positive space that embraces a different aspect of the site.

Creating Rooms: A Marriage of Inside and Out

From the beginning of the design, the space around a home should be considered to have as much roomlike potential as the major interior rooms. Use the form of the building to make its exterior space as positive and solid a thing as the building itself. If a house makes good livable rooms of the space around it, they will be used and, over the years, improved with as much intensity as any interior room. And, working together, the indoor and outdoor rooms can bring each other to life.

FOUR CORNERS *Exactly the opposite of the courtyard strategy, the house here occupies the center and creates a band of outdoor rooms around it, each playing a different role according to its position in the plan.*

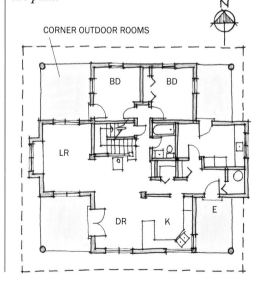

CORNER OUTDOOR ROOMS

More than any other single element, the form of the roof—as it is experienced on both the outside and the inside of a home—contains the meaning of shelter.

SHELTERING ROOF

This residence in the Napa Valley provides a pure expression of the pattern: A single, gabled roof flows smoothly into a wraparound porch, forming a powerful image of shelter.

WHATEVER ELSE IT IS, a house is fundamentally a place of shelter. Primitive homes were simply roofs on the ground, and the old expression "a roof over one's head" speaks to the very essence of home. The form of the roof, the way it contains and offers shelter to all the parts of the house, establishes the archetypal sense of the building as home. If a house does not use its roof to help form its exterior and does not let its roof give shape to any interior spaces, whatever other qualities it might possess, it never quite becomes a home.

Sheltering Roof suggests that, from its inception, we imagine a home as an inhabited roof, a roof whose form we experience both inside and out. Homes that suppress the shape of the roof, or simply tack one on above a flat ceiling, do not provide their residents with a basic sense of shelter. Such homes may successfully keep the weather out, but they fail to convey one of the distinct comforts of home— the *feel* of being enveloped by a simple, sloped-roof form.

INHABITING THE ROOF

A house in Berkeley, California, by architect Bill Mastin can help explain this pattern. The house is on a hillside site that slopes down and away from the street. The lot is narrow, and the slope faces north, so the architect had the formidable challenge of designing a house that would incorporate a two-car garage, entry, and south-facing open space all at the front of the building, hard against the street.

The projecting roofs and simple roof forms convey a feeling of shelter, the sense of the building as an "inhabited roof." The prominent gable makes a strong claim on our eye and visually crowns and centers the house.

Later in the book, the interiors of this house will be used to illustrate ideas about capturing natural light and graceful circulation. Here, the focus is on the way the roof form shapes the front of the house and, therefore, our initial experience of the house. The roof over the entry porch is exceedingly simple: a shed, sloping away from the building, toward the street, coming down low above the front door. This little shed seems to have cascaded down from the higher gable roof, centered over the balcony.

Stepping under the shed up to the front door, visitors find that the sense of shelter, of being gathered under this simple roof, is palpable. The thick garden wall, the low eaves, the sturdy-looking posts all work to this end. It is interesting that the garden wall opens at this point, allowing visitors to see its thickness and gain a glimpse into the walled and roofless south-facing garden court. Until you step up and *under* the porch roof, this outdoor room is seen only as a mysterious space behind a wall. In effect, once you're under its roof, the house begins to reveal itself, giving even this simple shedded space a strong sense of use and habitation.

At the second level, over the garage, there's a gable roof whose ridge is centered over a balcony. The gable visually seems to crown and center the house behind it, even though most of the house slopes down and away from this ridge and is not visible from the street. The doors centered below the

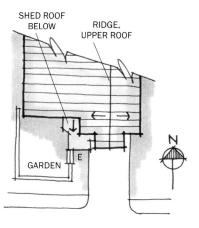

THE ROOF AS SYMBOL FOR HOME

The slope of a roof can be expressed in a great variety of ways. Relative steepness, shape, and material are all a matter of climate, tradition, and style; but the essence of this pattern is that the roof does slope and that the slope is experienced as containing the life of the building.

In the symbolic languages of nearly every culture there are instances of sloped roof form with deep associative meaning. In American Sign Language, for example, the sign for *home* begins with the sign for *roof*—two hands touching at the fingertips to form a gable. Similarly, the Chinese ideogram series for dwelling starts with a simple gable, and by adding a variety of symbols within, *roof* is transformed into "family," "peace," and "resting place." The ideogram for *cold* shows a roof sheltering a man on a mat with firewood.

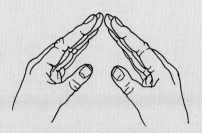

IN AMERICAN SIGN LANGUAGE, THE SIGN FOR HOME BEGINS WITH THE SIGN FOR ROOF.

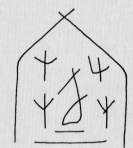

THE CHINESE IDEOGRAM FOR COLD

ridge tell us that the roof is lived in. As in a child's drawing of a house, the simple peaked roof speaks of home, suggesting a warm, enclosed space within. Stepping out on the balcony, residents again inhabit the roof, experiencing the intricate and beautiful framing above and around them. As with the entry overhang, the strong projection of the balcony roof, well beyond the front of the balcony, protects the space from south sun and storms and gives the whole building a memorable image of roof and shelter.

A CASCADING ROOF

In contrast to the down-sloping Berkeley house, the site of the Apter house in Oregon (see the photo at right), designed by Rob Thallon and Dave Edrington, reveals a great deal of the roof as we approach, providing another illustration of how this pattern works. In this case, the roof plan is made to follow the informal meanderings of the

The roof of this house informally follows its plan, cascading down the site, expressing the move from higher ceilinged common spaces to lower private ones.

ROOF PLAN FOLLOWS FLOOR PLAN
The floor plan responds to the site, following the dripline of the trees at the edge of the woods. The roof follows suit, gently stepping down the slope.

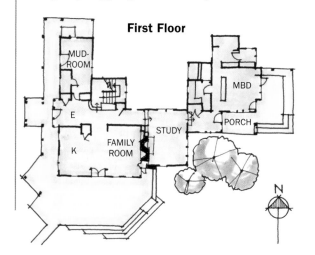

First Floor

MUD-ROOM

MBD

E

STUDY

PORCH

K

FAMILY ROOM

N

floor plan, laid out in response to the treeline of a forest to the north. The basic roof unit is a simple gable roof. But coupled with dormers and shaped to step down and around the site, this simple form creates a rich and lively shape.

The cascading form suggests the flow of the floor plan within, from the larger higher-ceilinged common spaces at the center of the house to the smaller and lower private ones at the edge. In this sense, the roof follows and expresses the intimacy flow of the house, placing the highest ceilings and roofs above the most public and populated rooms, and culminating in the low roof above the one-story master bedroom at the east end of the house with its private porch and study. The roof over the master bedroom forms a tiny habitable attic off the second-floor children's bedroom, and "hips out" to give shelter to the porch, a gesture that can be seen and felt from the interior.

The roof steps down toward the east, culminating in the roof over the master bedroom, which opens out to a sheltered porch.

78

The ceiling over the master bedroom is low and flat, in part to allow the higher attic space above to be inhabited by the children's bedroom. (The tiny gable-end window of the children's attic play space is visible in the photo on the facing page.)

WORKING WITH THE PATTERN

Whether the house is large or small, with simple or complex roof shapes, the roof should be visible and sloped, cascading down from high to low.

- *Fit the most important social spaces of the plan*—for example, entry, eating, bedrooms—to the roof. Let the form of the roof center these spaces, so that living in the house you feel as though, in some fashion, you are living in the roof.

- *Let the roof plan grow* from a traditional and elementary roof form, so that, by nesting, stretching, stacking, and compressing, a large house may be understood as a combination or transformation of a simple primitive roof.

- *Use a roof to mark the entry* and inform a visitor about the path into the house.

- *Make some spaces atticlike,* with the roof shape—perhaps even the roof frame—visible.

- *Make sure the roof can be experienced* from inside *and* outside. In some places, let it be high, visible, and beyond reach; in others, low, inviting, and touchable. Where possible, make spaces in and on the roof—roof gardens or terraces.

- *Use the naturally high and low portions* of the roof to create a variety of interior ceiling heights, with higher ceilings over larger spaces and lower ceilings over smaller spaces.

- *Use overhangs to shade and protect walls* and openings but also to create sheltered outdoor places and covered paths.

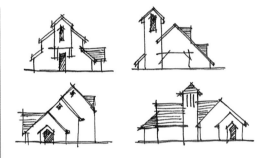

Larger homes can be compositions, combining and transforming simple roof forms.

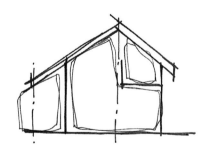

Use the naturally high and low portions of the roof to create a variety of interior ceiling heights and let the ceiling height variety reinforce the relative intimacy of each space.

A Roof to Live In

THE SPENCER RESIDENCE in Oakville, California, designed by William Turnbull Associates, perfectly captures this pattern with the simplest of means. The two-story, four-bedroom home is based on an almost-square plan shape with a barnlike gable roof, wraparound porch, and large dormers for the second-floor rooms. The main gable roof, with its 6-in-12 pitch, gives the house its basic form. The ridge of this roof, running east–west, establishes the highest and most dominant center for the building (and for the site). Reflected on the main floor plan of the house, this ridgeline becomes a centering axis, with fireplace at one end and main entry at the other. This is marked in the form of the roof by the tall chimneys at the opposite ends of the ridge. At the fireplace end, of course, the chimney houses the fireplace flue; at the entry end, it is a passive vent, shaped to match its opposite mate, in good proportion with the broad, steep roof.

The selection and treatment of materials clarifies the overall form of the roof. Finished with cedar shingles, it stands out sharply from the white-painted board-and-batten walls. As you approach the site, it is the powerful roof form that makes this building memorable. Etched against the rolling hills and pale blue sky of Napa Valley, the house is a roof to live in.

A ROOF TO LIVE IN *The main roof, a simple gable over an almost-square plan, centers and organizes the form of the house.*

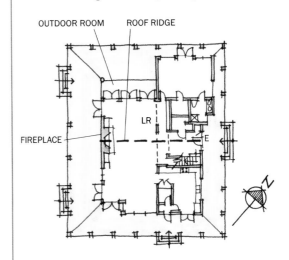

The roof ridge centers the fireplace, living room, and main entrance. Columns are spaced around the edge of the porch to create a subtle rhythm.

Looking back toward the kitchen and dining area, we see that the low ceiling off the larger central space forms a comfortable low edge to the high space. The ridge skylight, opposite the fireplace, reinforces the centrality of the main roof.

Everything follows from and is subordinated to the archetypal roof form.

*Make some spaces atticlike,
with the roof shape—perhaps
even the roof frame—visible.*

The porch forms a sheltered space around the entire house . . .

. . . widening at the western corner into a complete outdoor room. The round freestanding column marks the corner where the hipped lower roof turns and wraps around the building.

The roof slopes down to form a covered porch, supported by a series of wood posts that wrap around the entire building. And while the entire edge of the porch is formed by the marching posts and the elegant and uniform eaves line, the porch is slightly different on each side of the building. At the entry, it is 8 ft. deep and forms a sheltered entry porch. Following the porch clockwise, it becomes deeper at the rear of the building; and at the western corner, it becomes a complete outdoor room, adjacent and equivalent in scale to the living room. This north-facing space becomes a cool and shady oasis, a retreat during the region's hot summers. In addition to providing a sequence of functional living spaces, the wraparound porch gives the house a comfortable, vernacular character, a generous and spacious feel of shelter, a "great outdoors" safely within the roof.

EXPERIENCING THE ROOF INSIDE THE HOUSE

The impact of the roof form on the building continues inside the house. The main common space on the ground level is open to the full height of the roof, with the roof framing exposed. Within this space you feel the structure and are aware of the roof pushing up into the sky. Exposing roof framing on the interior is not essential to this pattern; a clean ceiling that traces the shape of the roof can be equally effective. Often, however, as in this house, the exposed framing can be used to give the house great character. And, as will be seen in COMPOSING WITH MATERIALS and PARTS IN PROPORTION, an exposed roof structure creates an opportunity to let the basic frame become a powerful part of the aesthetic experience of a home.

Out from the living room toward the west, the underside of the roof, which is visible through

From the living room, the full height and shape of the roof are experienced. At the conventional window and door height, the glazed wall permits a view out toward the horizon.

Climbing the stairs brings us closer to the roof and its visible framing, creating the feel of an elegant and spacious attic.

high transom windows, continues down and shelters the outdoor room and porch and protects the living room from the heat and glare of the west summer sun. Seeing it through the upper windows intensifies the feeling of the roof as a great sheltering tent. The effect is strengthened by the way the ceiling is framed. The coffered pattern, with its stained plywood over 2×4s over 2×10s, has the look of a refined and spacious attic. This becomes even more apparent as you climb the stairs and come closer to the roof frame and trusses.

To keep the large roof in proportion to the building as a whole and in particular to the main living space, it slopes down low at the edge of the porch. This slope prohibits a full ceiling height in the three upstairs bedrooms. To make these rooms habitable, to give them

The Spencer house is a powerful example of the Sheltering Roof pattern. But like all good houses it works on several levels and may be used to illustrate a number of other patterns:

Creating Rooms, Outside and In.
The broad roof overhang creates a necklace of outdoor rooms around the building. The most room-like is the space at the western corner of the porch, where the interior wall steps in.

Capturing Light.
Despite the broad roof overhang, all the main rooms of this house are flooded with balanced natural light; openings are located to draw in light from at least two directions. Natural light is used to wash walls, brighten corners, and, in general, reinforce the scale and character of the space.

Parts in Proportion.
The large main roof is the major element of the building, and it contains all the other major parts. Looking at the exterior, you can see that the dormers and chimney flues, while slightly over-scale by conventional standards, are perfectly balanced within the large roof. The wooden columns that ring the edge of the porch are sized and spaced to create a subtle rhythm.

Refuge and Outlook.
The upstairs bedrooms, tucked into the roof, are places of refuge. They are made all the more powerful by the oversize dormers cut through the roof. The dormers provide both a blast of natural light to these atticlike rooms and broad views out to the valley beyond.

Inside the bedrooms, where the main roof comes down to form the lowest spaces, the dormer windows penetrate the roof, creating higher ceilings than expected and further adding to the sense of inhabiting the roof.

light, and to continue the theme of the house as lived-in roof, the architect introduced three large dormers. From inside the rooms, the dormers seem even larger than expected and provide contrasting ceiling heights. The large windows that fill each dormer, free of the deep overhangs that contain the views from below, explode with light and view. Inside the low-ceilinged bedrooms, at the point of deepest refuge, the building opens up in a surprising way and gives its residents a grand experience of outlook, a window place that looks through and over the broad roof.

A Roof in Motion

THE ROOF OF THE SPENCER HOUSE is a geometric tour-de-force. Its beauty resides, in part, in the way everything is resolved within the single framework of "gable roof plus wraparound porch." Like the villas of Palladio, the house is an elegant object that exhibits precise rules of order, and these rules seem to give order or domain to the landscape around the building. The Aldermarsh house, by architect Ross Chapin—an equally striking example of the Sheltering Roof pattern—takes an entirely different approach.

The overall design strategy of the house is a sequence of ridges, shifting slightly from center to center, but all running in the same direction. This creates a zone of shelter between the dense, wooded grove and the open meadow to the south.

Looking through the bamboo grove and garden toward the breezeway and front door, you can see that the roof dominates the experience of arriving. As you pass through the dense, wild garden, the roof is the sheltered place ahead.

*Let the roof plan grow from a traditional
and elementary roof form, so that a large
house may be understood as a combination
or transformation of a simple primitive roof.*

A SHIFTING ROOFLINE

*The house is a sequence of connected parts,
from carport to private bedroom. Each of
the five parts is under its own gable roof.*

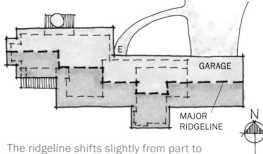

The ridgeline shifts slightly from part to
part to accommodate size and position.

In this view along the edge of the guest house, the
hip roof that wraps around the main building seems
to carve a shelter out of the woods.

Whereas the Spencer house is formal, shaping its parts within a single geometric framework, the Aldermarsh house is informal, more "home-grown." Using the same basic elements of gable roof and wrapping porch, it responds in a more ad hoc way to its site and its owners' needs. The basic strategy it employs is a sequence of 7-in-12 pitch gabled roofs, each roof over one of the five major parts of the house. In sequence from the point of arrival, the main parts are carport, guest house, breezeway, main house commons, main house private.

A ROOF FOR EACH PART

Each of the main parts has its own gable roof, and the ridge over each gable is allowed to shift slightly, in response to the area being covered and the need to connect each roof to its neighbor. The shifting ridge sequence creates a strong sense of movement in this plan. Whereas the previous house can be observed as a complete and single entity, this house is more about movement, the process of moving through it. (Chapin speaks of "choreography" when he reflects on the design process for this project.) As a result, while it is no less an example of the pattern than the Spencer house, the Aldermarsh house is more like a tiny village of roofs than a single, stand-alone house.

Another interesting difference between the two roof strategies is the way they relate to their sites. In the way it stands alone, the Spencer house, like the Italian villas from which it descends, seems to organize the site around it. The powerful symmetries created by its roof form stretch out into the site, generating invisible axes that order the site and provide a sense of orientation. The Aldermarsh house relates to its site more like the village architecture (particularly the traditional Japanese village) from which it descends. The building acts as a zone of transition between the two parts of the site: the dense garden and grove to the north, through which a visitor passes en route to the

As it moves toward the private bedroom and window seat that form the outermost edge of the house, the roof steps gently down toward the woods, creating lower and lower spaces within.

front door, and the open meadowlike lawn to the south. The house is located to define these two areas (in the manner of CREATING ROOMS, OUTSIDE AND IN).

The gable ridge is like a giant dashed line moving across the site, both defining and uniting the two places it creates. The two open areas are in many ways the grand spaces of the project, comparable, say, to the dramatic interior living space in the Spencer residence. The difference between the two houses becomes dramatically clear when we see how, at the very center of the Aldermarsh house sequence, the roof becomes simply a shelter over a breezeway and outdoor room. As you approach this space through the garden, the building "vanishes" and becomes a frame for the space beyond.

The lower roof edges also wrap around the corners of the building and provide a sheltering edge. But here again, the theme is movement. The outdoor room formed by the L-shaped main building is created by the deck. The roof overhang shelters the edge of the deck and cre-

At the breezeway, the "center of gravity" of the whole complex, the building itself recedes and becomes simply a powerful roof over an outdoor room. This roof room is both front door porch and gateway to the large south lawn. A broad south-facing section of the roof is translucent, flooding the space with light and revealing the frame of the roof.

The ceiling in the second-floor bedroom follows the roof framing, adding to the feeling of living under the roof. At the same time, the skylights take us past the roof to the outside.

ates a passage (like the traditional *engawa* in rural Japanese architecture) that wraps around the building, connecting the deck with the central breezeway.

The sequence of roofs comes to an end in the bedroom at the west end of the house. Like the cascading gables that ended in the master bedroom suite in the Apter house (see p. 78), this bedroom, with its roof, is the final space along the gradient of public to private; and it, too, ends in a low-roofed window place. In this case, the window seat looks out to an intimate view of the marshland that gives the house its name.

Once again, the house can be seen as an inhabited roof, the plan of the house growing directly out of the plan for the roof. The rooms above the first floor are tucked under the roof. And, like the dormers in the Spencer house, the skylights open up the rooms, give them head height, and blend the quality of shelter—being in and under—with the experience of looking out and beyond, through the roof.

The wraparound roof edge creates a passage, connecting a private deck to the public-entry breezeway. The deep overhang protects the wall and windows and provides a sheltered walk.

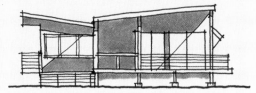

The Roof as Pavilion

The house from the east . . .

. . . and from the west. On the west, the roof extends out over the deck off the main room so that the principal common space is like one large pavilion, half-in, half-out.

THE PREVIOUS TWO HOUSES, while quite different in the way they are organized, both use the roof convention of high central ridge, down-sloping gable, and low edge. Now let's look at a project that, in response to site and climate, literally flips those relationships and yet provides a striking version of the pattern.

Pavilions, large-roofed, often open-air and tentlike structures, get their name from the Latin word *papilio* for "butterfly." It is the shape of the butterfly's wings, drawn partway down, that gives us the normal image of the sheltering pavilion. But we typically think of the butterfly with wings extended and up, and it is this image that gives us the term *butterfly roof*—a roof with two surfaces that rise from a low valley at their center to higher eaves at their edge. Architect Constance Treadwell's house in Hawaii is a true pavilion, because it is both an open-air, tentlike structure and a low-at-the-middle, wings-raised butterfly roof (complete with butterfly chairs!).

A SHELTERING PAVILION

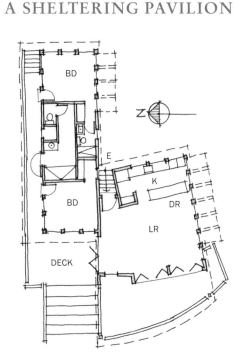

The two surfaces of the corrugated metal roof slope in toward the center at a pitch of 1.5 in 12, rising gently toward the edge, a shape that Treadwell describes as inspired by the image of "a delicate, winged insect alighting on the land." Another inspiration for the roof shape comes from the historic necessity in the arid climate of eastern Hawaii of using the roof surface to collect water. The butterfly roof channels the rainfall to one point and enables the owner to gather and use the 6 in. a year that falls on the broad roof of this one-story 1,500-sq.-ft. house.

A SHADY OPEN SPACE

The house consists of two parts, each with its own roof—a bedroom/bath wing and a commons, with kitchen and large main room and covered outdoor room. In a region where shelter means a protected, shady place with good ventilation, this roof strategy provides a high, open, and airy quality. The roof over the main room, springing from

With its wall/doors open, the main room and its covered deck are, in this climate, a perfectly sheltered yet open pavilion.

a height of about 9 ft. at the center and rising on its south edge to 11 ft., extends directly out from the room, whose western wall is essentially designed to fold back and disappear over a deck. This creates one large living space, which is half inside and half outside, the whole of it protected by the high floating roof above (compare this with PLACES IN BETWEEN).

Storm shutters are used both to protect the screened openings on the south side in bad weather and to form a kind of eave line, masking the view of the neighbors to the south and creating the look of a low sheltering edge in this otherwise open, high-ceilinged space.

The compelling sense of shelter this small house provides is perhaps most intensely experienced from the main room, first looking east through the kitchen and then west through the covered deck. The ceiling of the main room is exposed framing so the rafters above are visible, rising slightly toward the south. Outside the south window,

In this view through the main space to the outdoor room and its curved rail beyond, inside and outside merge into one shady protected place under the sheltering roof.

The shutters are repeated on the bedroom wing, where they protect the privacy of the easternmost bedroom.

All the features that make a sheltered pavilion of the large common spaces—the slight slope of the roof, the exposed framing, the exterior shutters—are compressed and repeated in the bedroom, where they create a nestlike room. Like the house itself, this is a room that is simultaneously protected and open.

the storm shutters slope down, a countervailing visual force. Looking west, through the open doors, the curve and slope of the roof join us to the landscape while sheltering us from it.

The bedroom wing is slipped back, and its roof shelters a walkway along the north edge of the building. The broad steps lead up to an open deck that connects the two wings. It is interesting that the architect does not connect these steps directly to the large roofed deck, requiring that residents first walk into the main room before going out to the covered space. This strengthens the sense of the covered deck as a room sheltered by the main roof.

In a climate with little rain and essentially no winter, this is a sheltering roof that turns roof conventions inside out, striking a wonderful balance between open and contained.

CAN A FLAT ROOF BE A SHELTERING ROOF?

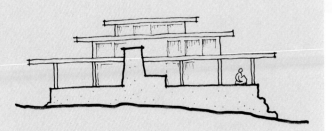

The sloped gable roof, high at the center, low at the edge, is archetypal in its connotation of home and shelter. It is the house that children draw over and over again, even when they have been raised in high-rise apartments.

The so-called "modern movement" in architecture, which grew out of Europe after World War I, avoided pitched-roof buildings, deep overhangs, and exposed roof framing almost as a matter of principal. The modernist style found virtue in flat roofs, glazed walls, and open plans. Many architects of this period did find ways to reconcile the language of modernism with the traditional pattern of sheltering roof. In the Los Angeles residential work of Schindler and Neutra, for example, the roof is often expressed as a broad surface, floating on columns across glazed walls, sheltering outdoor terraces and decks (see the drawing above). The broad eaves create a sense of shelter, and the exposed beams suggest strength and reliability.

The great hero in the reconciliation of flowing modernist space and traditional roof form was Frank Lloyd Wright, whose Prairie-style homes, with their near-flat roofs, combine powerful images of shelter and open, free-flowing space. But more often in modernist homes the pattern was neglected. Roofs were simply the tops of boxes, invisible from the outside, indistinguishable from the ceiling within.

In his book *Lived-In Architecture,* Phillippe Boudon examined the houses in Pessac, France, built by Le Corbusier shortly after World War I. These houses, intended for a working-class neighborhood, were early milestones of the modern movement—concrete, sharply delineated forms, flat roofs. Fifty years later, Boudon found the houses completely transformed by the succession of occupants. Everyone, it seems, had converted his modernist dwelling into something more like a traditional home. Wide windows had been replaced with narrow, small-paned windows; open terraces had been covered; sheds had been added; and, in many cases, flat roofs had been replaced with a variety of pitched roofs. Many of the renovations were practical, but it is striking to note that the "language" of the homes had been changed. The additions made the houses less the "machines to live in" that Le Corbusier imagined and more like the inhabited, sheltering roofs of the preindustrial homes of the region.

FROM MODERNIST CUBE TO SHELTERING ROOF

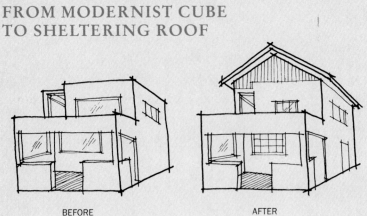

BEFORE

AFTER

A CLUSTER OF SHELTERING ROOFS

To conclude this pattern, let's look at two large homes that manage their scale by creating a cluster of sheltering roofs. The first home, in Wyoming, takes its inspiration from the rustic log dwellings built by homesteaders in the region. These are simple, sturdy buildings that descend from traditional Scandinavian farmhouses. Architect John Carney's approach to this 4,100-sq.-ft. home was to develop three major ridgelines, descending from the two-story west wing, through a connecting middle wing, to the one-story east wing. Each major roof has smaller shed and gable dormers subordinated to it, used to mark special places in the plan.

The inside spaces reveal a variety of ways to inhabit the roof. The central building houses a living room, open to the interior of the gable form with its timber trusses—a large, refined barn right at the heart of the cluster. Even the flat-ceilinged spaces express the sheltering roof above. For example, the ceiling framing in the screened porch off the kitchen (see the photo on p. 96) aligns with the frame for the windows and bays, which gives it the feel of a nook tucked under the roof.

INSPIRATION FROM THE PAST

Like the Wyoming home, a Colorado residence by architect Larry Yaw draws its inspiration from local vernacular buildings with roots in European traditions (see the photos on p. 97). In this case, the forms and materials of Rocky Mountain towns are married to the courtyard hillside strategies of Provence, in southern France. On a

Each of the three major roofs includes dormers and sheds. The whole ensemble cascades down from the west wing with its central dormer to the east wing with its low window bay.

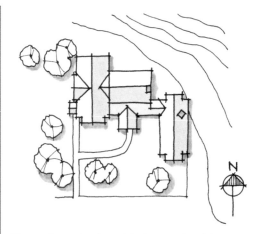

The roof plan begins with three major ridges, linked to form a single cascade of roofs.

In the middle wing, the living room is a barnlike space. Its ridge is not the highest in the roof plan; but from the interior, it is experienced as such, the center of the cluster.

Even the flat-ceilinged porch off the kitchen of the Wyoming residence continues the pattern. The exposed ceiling and wall framing are proportioned and aligned to give this sheltered place a sense of order and calm.

CLUSTERED AROUND A COURT *The major ridgelines roughly follow the court—except for the tower and arched opening, which center the whole complex.*

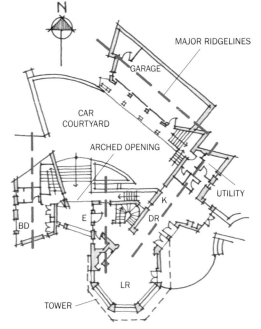

small benched site that overlooks a meadow with mountains beyond, Yaw has created an entry court—a room in the manner of the pattern CREATING ROOMS, OUTSIDE AND IN—by arranging a cluster of roofs that simultaneously shape the court and focus the spaces they shelter out toward the view beyond. A study of the major ridgelines gives a clue as to how this has been accomplished.

The ridges follow the perimeter of the court in a predictable way, along the eastern dining/kitchen wing, turning at the garage, and turning again at the western bedroom wing. Then at the main entry on the south side of the court the architect has injected an element of surprise. The entry is both a deep, sheltering, shady arch that gives the visitor approaching the front door a glimpse of the vast view beyond, and a tower, rising to the highest point around the courtyard and terminating in a simple gable oriented toward the view. This form, a powerful image of shelter, at the southern edge of the court, contains both the low sheltered front door and the high point from which the entire roof form flows.

Even in these large houses, the architect is building a cluster from the simple traditional gable shapes. The roofs combine to create a complex set of visible sloped forms, tracing a movement from high to low. The most important social spaces of the plan are fit into the roof form, and the roof is allowed to center these spaces—so that those living in the house feel as if, in some fashion, they are living in the roof.

Sheltering Roof:
A Primary Pattern of Home

For a house to convey the meaning of home, its roof must be more than something tacked on, something applied after the two-dimensional plan of the building had been designed. Think of the roof as a volume that can be experienced outside and in. From the outside, whether it is simple and traditional or unusual and complex, the roof form should center and organize the overall shape and sequence of the house. From the inside, the interior shape of the roof should resonate throughout the house, from the entry to the largest common rooms through to the smallest private nooks.

This form, a powerful image of shelter, at the southern edge of the court, contains both the low sheltered front door and the high point from which the entire roof form seems to descend. The stone wall becomes deep and sheltering, protecting the occupants and opening the enclosed court to the view beyond.

The building is made from a collection of sheltering roof forms informally linked around a courtyard. The court is a rough rectangle, with a curve inscribed that feels like it's the arc of a larger circle. The resulting shape is a positive, enclosing shape, but one that also contains a hint of the vast circular bowl of space that is the high meadow beyond.

A house should be shaped in response to the sun, with its rooms located and organized so that all important spaces receive abundant and balanced light.

CAPTURING LIGHT

Light can direct and enhance our movement through space. Centered under a large skylight, this stair is brightened by a wash of light down the north wall; as the stair turns we are drawn first to the large glazed wall of the dining room (the source of the light falling across the wall to the right) and then to the view through the large window to the east.

People are comfort-loving creatures. We turn toward the sun, seeking light and warmth, needing it to nourish both spirit and body. The position of the sun in the sky, the color of its light, keeps us in touch with the time of day and the season of the year. The amount and type of cloud cover connect us to changes in the weather. While artificial light illuminates the dark, the impact of natural daylight has a completely different effect on our experience. The intensity of sunlight is so great that no artificial light can approach it, and it offers a complete color spectrum that is not present in most standard artificial lighting. With the light comes warmth, heating the objects it strikes and the spaces it fills. When we build homes it is important to locate and organize them in a way that allows all important spaces to receive abundant natural light. This single step probably has more effect on our perception of comfort than does any other aspect of home design.

If light is essential, shadow is the complement that gives it power. Relentless light (imagine a fluorescent-lit classroom or a discount store) deprives a space of the meaning that comes with variety. Pools of bright light draw us to them because they highlight an area within a surrounding of shade. Shadowy corners or edges lend an air of mystery to a well-lit interior. Retreating into the shade when the sun is high allows us to enjoy a cool space on a hot day. And filtering sunlight—mixing light with shadow—to admit just the right amount

As the sun moves from east to west, the heat of the day increases and with it the need for shading of windows and doors.

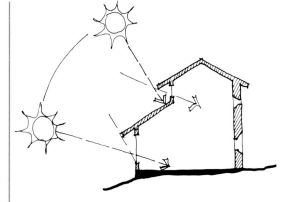

In summer, when the sun is high in the sky, the windows are protected from heat gain by the deep eaves; however, the low winter sun is able to enter the house.

allows us to select the appropriate intensity of light for any activity. It is the play of light and shadow that gives shape to forms and brings life to our surroundings.

WORKING WITH THE PATTERN

Effectively capturing natural light requires planning at several scales. It is a process that begins with the selection of the site and must continue through to final details of window design and shading. Here are some key guidelines for this pattern:

- *Locate the house on the site* so that it receives light throughout the day.

- *Shape the house so that light can enter* every important room from at least two sides to create a balance.

- *When light from a second side* is not possible, allow for light from above through skylights or clerestory windows.

- *Plan the placement of rooms* so that each space receives light at a suitable time of day for the activities that occur there.

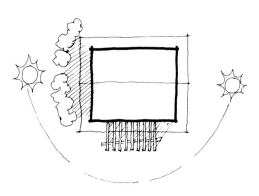

- *Shape and size each opening* to suit both the climate and the activities that will be lit from the window.

- *Plan the details of design* and installation to relate windows to the character of the house as a whole.

- *Create window places*—bays, dormers, window seats—to enhance the life of the house.

- *Use shading devices to control* the amount of light and heat that enters the house.

LOCATING AND SHAPING THE HOUSE

In the pattern INHABITING THE SITE, we looked at the role of light in locating and shaping the house. It is essential to understand how different solar orientations affect the light the building receives. In the northern hemisphere, as the sun rises, eastern light fills the sky, the sun is low, and east-facing windows receive direct light. Morning activities—awakening, breakfast, bathing—are enhanced by sun exposure as the body responds to daylight by becoming more alert. In most climates mornings are cool, overheating is not a big concern, and east-facing windows can admit light with minimum need for solar protection (see the top drawing on the facing page). By midmorning, summer sun is higher in the sky; and overhead shading devices begin to protect the glass from direct light; yet in winter the lower arc of the sun allows light to continue to enter, providing natural warmth.

Southern light is higher in the sky in summer than in winter. Deep overhangs or screens above south-facing windows capitalize on this difference to keep the midday sun out during the hottest months but to allow heat gain in the winter. Shading devices, when carefully planned based on the building's geographic location, can have a major impact on the building's thermal comfort and still provide light and view. Trellises with deciduous vines, sun shades with angled louvers, and tall deciduous trees planted on the south side can all contribute.

On Bainbridge Island in Washington State, architect Marc LaRoche designed a long, thin south-facing house. To moderate the intense summer sun, he incorporated a long terraced porch on the south side that provides protection for the large windows and glazed doors and forms a sequence of usable outdoor spaces. Transom windows run above the doors and windows, giving the entire south wall a great sense of openness and allowing reflected light from the porch ceiling

Light filtered through the vine-covered open framing at the edge of this roof softens the bright midday sun, creating an inviting shaded spot on hot days. In the winter, the combination of fallen leaves and a lower sun angle allows midday light to fill the same spot, creating a protected sunny pocket.

LIGHT FROM TWO SIDES

Placing the house on the site to take best advantage of available light requires a study of the light and shadow patterns created by surrounding structures, by the topography, and by landscape elements. As the house takes shape, a primary goal is to bring light into each room from two sides, a strategy that reduces glare within the room and gives each room sun exposure through a good portion of the day. This can be accomplished in many ways.

In a simple rectangular house (see below), each corner room has the potential for windows on two sides. A long thin house and a house shaped with long wings afford the possibility of windows on opposite walls. Homes tightly fitted between surrounding buildings can achieve light on two sides by using an inner courtyard and bringing in light from above.

LONG THIN HOUSE *The long thin house allows light to enter from opposite sides of most rooms.*

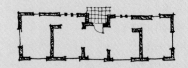

WINGS OF LIGHT *A house with wings assembles pieces of the long thin house form to create rooms with the potential for light on two or three sides.*

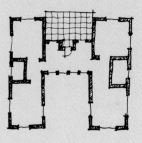

FOUR-SQUARE HOUSE
The simple four-square house allows light into two sides of each corner room.

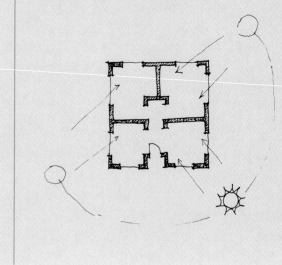

ATRIUM HOUSE WITH LIGHT MONITORS *On sites where security concerns or building codes limit exterior windows, the combination of a central atrium and light monitors or skylights can create balanced light, by bringing it down from above.*

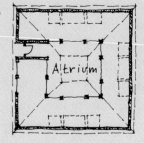

to enter the house (see the photo below). To bring direct sunlight into the center of the house, the architect used a long dormer sheltering clerestory windows. The rhythm of the posts that support the edge of the porch is matched by that of the brackets that support the dormer's overhang—helping to filter the sun and provide an interesting shadow pattern on the exterior walls and inside the building.

Western light needs to be managed; as the sun gets low in the sky, west-facing windows receive nearly horizontal rays of light that enter below roof eaves or sun shades. On summer afternoons, the sun can be too warm: Excluding it requires a barrier that comes between the window and the sun, blocking out views as well as light. Landscape elements such as trees to the west can provide seasonal protection, or west-facing windows may require adjustable window coverings: awnings, drop shades, adjustable louvers, and shutters all offer control over the amount of light admitted.

The north side of the building is a special case; it receives almost no sun and so offers no opportunity for solar heat gain. Artists and craftspeople, however, value north light for its even quality and the consistent color rendering it offers. Windows on this side of the house tend to be a major source of heat loss, so in most climates it is best to use them carefully. In homes planned to conserve energy, the north wall is often treated as an insulating barrier filled with service rooms such as closets and bathrooms. Where windows are required, they are small and may be curtained to protect against cold.

Even the most difficult sites can effectively capture light. On an urban site in Seattle, a home designed by Tom Bosworth (already introduced in Pattern One) turned the conventional design inside out. Because the site is quite narrow, Bosworth filled it from side to side, organizing all the rooms around an inner court (see the drawing on p. 104).

The high clerestory windows in this kitchen/dining area fill the room with soft light and allow walls to be used for storage and display. Protected by eaves from the hot summer sun, these south-facing windows do not create hot spots or glare on work surfaces.

*When light from a second side is not possible,
allow for light from above through skylights
or clerestory windows.*

LIGHT FROM THE CENTER

*On tight sites, an innovative plan strategy is
to wrap the house around an open space.
Light then comes from the center of the
house—the atrium—and finding sources of
balancing light becomes a design challenge.*

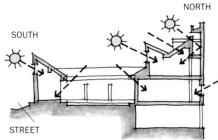

First Floor

Second Floor

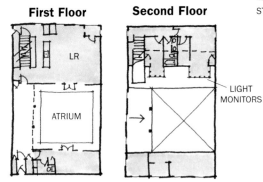

LR

ATRIUM

LIGHT
MONITORS

Shaping the roof to admit light can
solve difficult problems presented by
site or location. Here, the shed roof
reaches up to bring in southern light
along the street without compromis-
ing privacy at the front of the site.
To the north, a combination of dormers and clerestory windows project
above the roof to gather light.

Even under difficult circumstances, it can be possible to capture light from two sides. In this Seattle
house, the upper floor is a space within the roof; light
comes from a combination of glassy light-monitor
dormers on the south and clerestory windows higher
on the roof that allow light to wash the north wall.

The outer walls on the sidelines of the property could not have windows at the lower floor because of security concerns and building
codes that prohibited openings close to the property line, but the
inner court is essentially a light well, filled with large windows. And
north-facing windows open to the back of the site. On the second
floor, Bosworth achieved balanced light using a combination of high
light monitors on the south and clerestory windows to the north that
bring in light from above.

Another major goal in shaping a house is to ensure that each room
receives light at the time of day that is most appropriate. Planning
for morning light in the bedrooms and the kitchen or breakfast room
gets the day off to a sunny start. At noon, areas of the house that
are active—a home office, the family room, the table where lunch is
eaten—will be enlivened by sun in the winter but may require shade
in the summer. A window that looks toward the sunset but can be
shaded will enhance the late afternoon to evening hours. Each family
lives in its home in a unique way and should plan windows to support individual patterns of activity that occur throughout the day.

The major source of light in this guest room is the wide door opening to the atrium; on the street side, light is balanced and privacy is maintained by placing a window high on the wall, well above passersby.

PLACING AND SIZING WINDOWS

Interior light quality is strongly influenced by the size, style, and location of windows, glazed doors, and skylights. Strategies for sizing and placing these openings through the wall vary greatly and are heavily influenced by climate and by weather conditions. In cold northern areas with long winters, it is critical to conserve heat; and windows tend to be smaller, recessed within thick and heavily insulated walls and sometimes protected against storms or snow. Traditional New England homes with small, deep-set, shuttered windows epitomize this approach. When cold climates and energy concerns limit the area

Splaying the walls in this dormer window allows the light to travel along the surface, framing the view of the woods seen beyond the stovepipe.

of openings, locating the windows effectively to ensure enough light in every room becomes very important. Each window has the potential to be a key feature in the room and to create a special place nearby that takes advantage of the pool of light spilling through.

At a residence in northern California by architect George Homsey, windows are grouped to surround a wood-burning stove (see the photos at left). The bay window behind the stove looks into a wooded forest, allowing the family to enjoy the view of the outdoors and the fire simultaneously. Because the bay projects beyond the wall it has windows on three sides, increasing light and view. Above the bay, a dormer frames the chimney pipe and reflects light down to the room below and into the second-floor loft—using one window to bring light to both levels. (More of this house can be seen in Pattern Eight.)

Warm tropical climates demand a different approach to window design; walls dissolve as floor-to-ceiling panes of glass open the interior to the outside. Shade to control heat gain becomes more important, and screening of openings plays a critical role in planning. Cross-ventilation may be essential, and a deep overhang to protect open windows during rainstorms is a design concern.

There is often a tension between the desire to sit around a fire and the equally strong desire to look out at the view. That conflict is resolved here by placing a woodstove within a window bay. The connection to the view of the woods outside is reinforced by composing with materials: tree trunks, stripped of bark, frame the stove and support the beam above.

WHERE DO THE WINDOWS GO?

Window placement and the quality of light that enters a home are significantly affected by climate.

In Cool Climates . . .

- Windows placed high in the wall so that they "see the sky" admit indirect bright light and allow it to penetrate deeply into the room. The brighter the light outside (sky, a reflective wall, light bouncing off water or snow), the smaller the required opening.

- Splayed window jambs and sills admit more light—both by not blocking light rays at the perimeter of the window and by using the angle of the window reveal to bounce the light that enters the room.

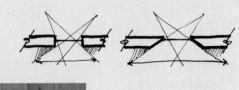

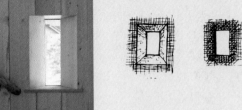

- Windows or skylights placed so that one edge is continuous with the adjoining wall or ceiling allow light to flow along the surface, creating a glow rather than the dark edge between light and shadow.

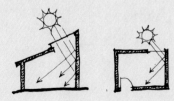

SECTION   PLAN

In Warm Climates . . .

- Think of glazed doors as large windows. Walls of glass that slide or fold to open to adjacent decks can extend both the visual and the usable space of the house.

- Provide very deep overhangs or add awnings to keep hot summer sun out of south-facing windows.

- Carefully plan or limit windows facing east or west, which will admit the low horizontal light of morning or evening. Capitalize on existing landscaping or provide sun-blocking barriers outside these windows. Recognize that anything that blocks the light of the setting or rising sun will also block views, so plan accordingly.

- Use indirect light where possible. Light bounced off of baffles or surfaces outside the building will not increase heat as direct light does.

- Screens may be essential, but they also have a real impact on clarity of vision. Locate important view windows where screens are not required. Consider the screen style when planning the windows. Sliding screens may stack to the side; roll-down screens can disappear. Screens should be operable or easily removable for window cleaning.

Plan windows so that direct light is admitted only from the north or early in the morning.

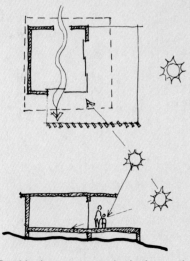

Provide deep eaves to shade the southern sun and vertical screens or plantings to protect west-facing openings.

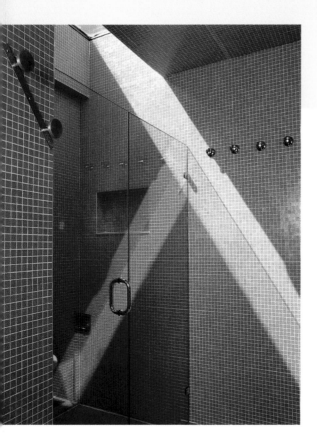

Light from the skylight plays on the blue tile and reflects through drops of water, heightening the bathing experience in this shower designed by Harry Bates.

LIGHT FROM ABOVE

While windows at eye level can provide view as well as light and offer a wider variety of shading options, there are many situations in which it is desirable to bring light into a space from above. For rooms in the center of the house, a skylight may be the only option; in locations such as the shower shown at left, the skylight creates dramatic light in a setting with complete privacy. The clerestory windows of the Seattle house, shown earlier (pp. 104–105), are a good example of the use of an opening high in a room to balance the light from windows on the opposite side. To create a dramatic shaft of light or to fill a narrow space with light, high openings are ideal.

Light from above can take many forms; in its simplest form it can be a "hole" in the roof, a skylight protected by a glazed cover. Light from overhead tends to be quite bright in daytime so the way in which skylights are placed has a real impact on the way the space below is experienced. In rooms with vaulted ceilings, a skylight can be perceived as a very bright spot against a dark surrounding—a perception that will be less apparent if light reflects off nearby surfaces. When the opening is located at the edge of a room, the light

HOLE WITH SHAFT OF LIGHT

will wash down the wall brightening that side of the room. A light shelf placed below a skylight will bounce light back onto the ceiling, and a ridge skylight—one that sits right at the peak of the ridge in a room with vaulted ceilings—allows light from one side of the ridge to flow down along the opposite ceiling. All of these strategies result in a brighter space with less glare.

WALL WASH

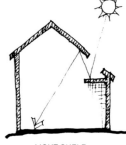

LIGHT SHELF

In spaces with attics above, it is necessary to create a shaft through the attic to

The clerestory window in this Berkeley home plays several important roles. It marks the center of the house; provides light at the circulation crossroads; and, by forming a tower with interior "windows" at the building's center, balances light in the living areas.

RIDGE

conduct light to the space below. The minimal version of the shaft is the commercially available light tube—a reflective conduit for light that ends in a skylight much like a domed surface-mounted ceiling light. A softer light can be created by placing a flat diffusing panel with obscure glass at the plane of the ceiling below a skylight. A more dramatic approach uses the attic area to form the

LIGHT TUBE

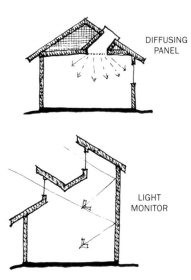

DIFFUSING
PANEL

LIGHT
MONITOR

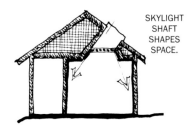

SKYLIGHT
SHAFT
SHAPES
SPACE.

shaft to shape space in the room below. Light monitors, dormers, and clerestory windows are all strategies for bringing light in through the roof while using a conventional window; they combine some of the shading potential of windows with the freedom of placement possible with skylights.

SHAPING AND DETAILING WINDOWS

Bringing in light is not the only role that windows play; much of the character of a house comes from its windows. Architects use horizontal bands of windows to identify the Bauhaus style, and the Palladian window is a major element in classical buildings. Double-hung windows tend to look traditional, and aluminum sliders suggest suburban ranch house.

Windows can define style or they can work against it. Divided lights fracture the view and enhance the sense of being *in*, whereas large sheets of glass that reach from floor to ceiling blur the distinction between in and out. Windows placed asymmetrically on a façade create a very different home than one with equally spaced small windows or a centered assembly of windows. Windows that pop out evoke a different response from those that are recessed or simply set flush. The shape, the operation, the glazing, the assembly, and the details of the surround of windows tell us a great deal about a house. Carefully planned, they feel of a piece with the house, very visible elements that carry the mood of the whole.

Most windows don't just admit light; they allow us to look out and others to see in. Inevitably, there is a conflict in some locations between the desire for light or view and the need for privacy. High windows or skylights address this problem—but when windows are needed, planning is required. Many of the conventional solutions, such as curtains and shades, offer privacy but restrict the amount of light or the quality of the view when they are in place. Use of obscure glazing is a traditional solution where restricting the view is essential.

A skylight at the peak brings light and drama to this pyramid-shaped space.

The desire for a light-filled entry combined with the need to minimize views into the house led to the design of this window wall for a home in Santa Barbara, California, by Robert du Domaine. Mixing different obscure and clear glass panes in a divided-light wood window creates a mosaic of light patterns indoors. Occasional clear panes allow views out and up, but careful placement limits looks in.

It also offers a second advantage: The light quality through obscured glass can be wonderful, a general glow, offering only veiled or screened hints of what lies beyond. Designers use special glazing—sandblasted glass, striped patterns, glass block—to filter undesirable views out, to control views in, and to establish stylistic themes.

At every step of designing a home, from the selection of the building site down to the final detailing of materials, the gathering of light influences our decisions. And in remodeling an existing structure, the greatest impact can often be achieved by opening a wall or a ceiling to bring in more light. Let's now look at two houses in different parts of the country that take very different approaches to capturing light.

A House That Follows the Sun

THE JACOBS FAMILY came to architect Tut Bartzen with an exceptional site, part of a larger family lot that they hoped would help them meet their goal of building a light-filled home closely related to the outdoors.

Located on a bluff in Rhode Island with a full southern exposure, the site enjoys a distant view of the ocean to the southwest and visual privacy created by the trees and slopes surrounding the building. Given complete freedom to position the house so that each space could enjoy light at the time of day it would be most valuable, the Jacobses planned the location of each room and outdoor space carefully. They recognized that this required a good understanding of all the activities they planned, when and where those activities would take place, and sensitivity to the light requirements for each.

SHAPING THE HOUSE

The owners wanted a practical house, one that took full advantage of the light and the spectacular views and one that allowed ease of movement from indoors to out. In keeping with its New England setting, the basic form of the house is straightforward—a two-story rectangle with cut-away chamfered corners facing south. The small size and simple form allow windows on two sides of every room, which balances the light in the rooms, reducing the glare that comes with looking toward a single light source. It also allows better light control—shading one window to control heat gain or to increase privacy does not require dimming the entire room.

The house is carefully positioned on the site. By setting the house with its leading corner facing south, two full sides of the building receive south sun, filling the interior with light from morning until night. A wide porch—a perfect example of PLACES IN BETWEEN—with a balcony

South-facing outdoor spaces on two levels ensure a wide variety of seating options on sunny days. The porch shades windows on the lower level during the summer months.

Light from the stair landing helps balance light in the living areas below and the library hall above.

For those who want full
sun the upper balcony
offers comfortable seating
and a long view.

THE PATH OF THE SUN

*Siting the building diagonally to the
south takes maximum advantage of
available sunlight. Every room gets
direct sun at some point during the day,
and the living room and master bedroom
above get sun from morning till evening.*

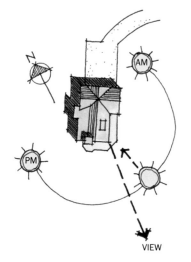

VIEW

above wraps the south corner, inviting an easy flow from the living
room, entry, and bedrooms out toward the view. The porch roof provides natural seasonal light control for the lower floor, limiting the
entry of light when the sun is high in the sky at midday in summer.
When the sun is lower in the sky—early morning and evening, winter,
spring, and fall—the angle allows light to penetrate the porch and
enter the rooms beyond. As the day or the season gets cooler, the sunlight reaches deeper into the house.

  With a roofed porch on the lower level and a fully exposed balcony above, there's always a wide range of sun exposure options
available; sunbathers or shade seekers can follow the sun's path
throughout the day.

FOLLOW THE LIGHT

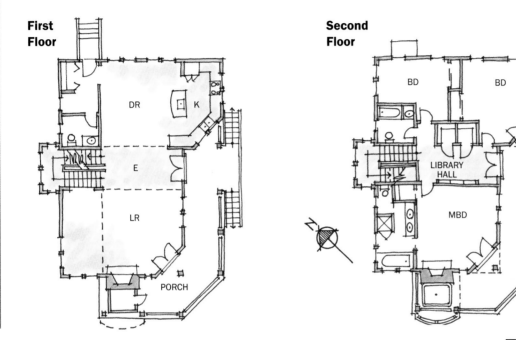

First Floor

Second Floor

LIGHT TO MOVE TOWARD

Light is attractive. We naturally move toward it. We feel more secure when we can really see our surroundings and safer when we know what is happening around us. Curiosity and comfort-seeking draw us toward windows and encourage us to settle at the edge of well-lit areas. Careful placement of openings can use the attraction of light to define the circulation system of the building. Under its skin of porches and balconies, the Jacobs house is an efficient, compact box with a center entry that divides rooms to each side.

In THE FLOW THROUGH ROOMS, we discuss the importance of creating a well-defined circulation pattern that moves along the edge of common areas and accesses private areas economically. This home is a perfect example of a very straightforward approach. The center hall joins the front door and the stairway directly ahead, funneling activity along the edge of the common areas and creating a "travel zone" at the center of the building. Natural light at each end of this

The quality and control of light are important for outdoor spaces as well as for interiors. The porch here creates a deep band of shade at midday in summer but allows light to enter when the sun is low in the sky.

Windows on three sides fill this stair landing with light, creating an inviting place to walk toward or to stop and linger.

zone—at the landing where the stair turns, and at the pair of doors that open out to the porch—gives clarity to the circulation pattern, while larger pools of light in the rooms to the side draw us toward sitting areas. Upstairs, the central circulation pattern is repeated. A wide hall links the top of the stairs with French doors opening to the upper balcony. Bookshelves line the side of the hall, inviting us to linger, and doors to bedrooms and bathrooms open to the sides. Generous light and open space make this a pleasant place to be, not just to pass through.

FOLLOWING THE SUN

Creating a house suitable for informal entertaining was an important goal for the owners. The large open living, dining, and kitchen area on the lower floor, connected to a generous outdoor living area on the porch, meets this requirement. It also allows an arrangement of rooms that flow together and capture the sun's light from morning to night. Because the house is small, every room has a corner location, which allows light to enter from two sides. Upstairs, each of the three bedrooms has windows to the east; as the sun comes up it gradually fills the rooms with light, waking the occupants gently. Each bedroom also has windows on a second wall, balancing the light in the room and increasing the period of direct sunlight.

At breakfast, the eastern sunlight enters the kitchen and adjoining dining room. Diners start the day with the early warmth of morning sun balanced by light from the kitchen window to the south. By noon, the warm midday sun strikes the south face of the building, with its chamfered corners oriented to the view. A long wraparound porch shades the south side on the lower floor, giving midday protection to a kitchen window that fills the south-facing wall and to the

The southeast-facing window and dormer in this master bedroom ensure that sleepers know when the sun has risen. Windows to the southwest create a balanced light.

Looking across the dining room, we see the large northeastern windows. They provide soft light, which mixes with the strong light streaking in from the south and eliminates the potential glare that would otherwise be experienced by someone sitting at the dining table.

The high ceilings in this living room allow space for transom windows above the glazed doors and windows that fill walls on three sides. The result is an unusually bright and open space that changes mood as the sun moves from east to west.

French doors that open from the living room to the porch. (Because the porch faces south, it offers a deep band of shade in the summer, when the sun is high in sky; the winter sun is low enough to fill the porch and the rooms beyond with light.) By late afternoon, the sun has moved around to the west and enters through the corner windows of the living room. When the low sunlight shines into these windows, which are exceptionally high (10 ft. to the top of the transom), it penetrates deeply into the room.

Upstairs, the floor plan is organized to emphasize morning light in the bedrooms; by mid-afternoon, the bedrooms are protected from heat gain by the placement of the bathroom and fireplace to the west. Downstairs, it is important for afternoon and evening activities to have a sense of the light but also to be protected from heat gain. Here the protection is created by dense landscaping outside the corner windows, which blocks the sun as it gets low in western sky. The west-facing corner of the stairwell landing has windows that bounce light onto the very center of the house, where it falls down the stairs and into the entry hall—a balance to the more direct western light.

THE SHADY SIDE

Just as moss grows on the north side of trees because of the lack of direct sun, the north side of a building is always the coolest, most damp spot. Locating service spaces with lower light requirements such as bathrooms, storage, mudroom, and laundry on the north side helps a house in several ways. It preserves the south side for rooms with light-intensive needs, it locates the smallest windows on the wall where the heat loss through windows is highest, and it saves energy by creating an insulating band of spaces that can be closed off against the cooler north wall. At the Jacobs house, the mudroom, closets, and powder room fill the northern corner of the lower floor, forming a buffer to the cold.

In this almost traditional home, several strategies combine to create a house that is filled with light. Ceilings are high, and double-hung windows with transoms above reach almost to the ceiling. The large rooms and open plan of the south side allow light to penetrate deep into the center of the house, warming it early in the day and through the winter. The house itself is sited so that it has excellent solar access until late afternoon, when it capitalizes on the existing tree cover to avoid heat gain. The room layout is planned to follow the sun and uses careful placement of conventionally styled windows that fit comfortably with the brown-shingle building. While the Jacobs home succeeds because it effectively capitalizes on a great site and expands on local building styles, the Mackota house in California, which we'll look at next, sits on a difficult site in a neighborhood with no unified sense of appropriate building style.

PATTERNS IN CONTEXT

While the Jacobs house is an excellent example of a home designed to gather light, its power as a building comes from the interaction of many patterns.

Inhabiting the Site.
On large sites, finding the best location can be a challenge. Here, the house is located toward the north edge of the site, against the edge of a large clearing. This approach places the house at the rim of a very large, south-facing outdoor room (Creating Rooms, Outside and In) and offers excellent solar exposure from morning to night.

The Flow through Rooms.
This house is a classic example of a very efficient centralized travel pattern that moves along the edges of common areas on the lower floor and treats the wide upper hallway as a library, enlivened by the French doors opening to the upper balcony.

Refuge and Outlook.
The porch on the lower floor offers a classic outlook—a view from on high to the ocean about a mile away—and provides refuge in the protected southern corner of the porch, which is raised above the ground, deep within the shadow, and tucked behind the railing.

Places in Between.
The porch that wraps around the south-facing corner of the building is a perfect place in between—sheltered from the weather but exposed enough to be clearly outside rather than in. More enclosed is the stair landing, a bay with windows on three sides that is both between floors and between indoors and out. It invites us to pause.

Changing Light for a Difficult Site

POSITIONING A BUILDING on the site so that each room faces the desired light exposure is ideal, but it's often not possible. Adjacent buildings, unusual topography, landscape features, and zoning restrictions can all have a major impact on how a house is positioned on its site—and on the location and type of openings that are possible. When Richard Mackota asked our firm to design his new home, he brought a very different set of design circumstances from that used for the Jacobs house. The lot he had purchased was one of many left

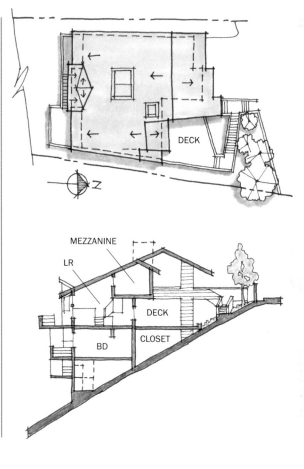

Located on a steep down slope, the south face of the house has no natural protection from the midday sun. Deep eaves and projecting decks with a horizontal railing system create shade for the windows below, while an electrically operated screen can be dropped over the outside of the large window.

Careful placement of openings can ensure that the center of a house is filled with light. Here, a skylight brings a shaft of light into the stairwell, and an interior window above the doorway into the kitchen lets light flow through into the dining room.

Light floods down this stairwell from the skylight high above; because the stairs are in the center of the building, they bring light to the inside of each room they serve, creating a balance with the light from perimeter windows.

Protected from the wind and warmed by early morning light, the lower patio is tucked between house and street, an outdoor room enlivened by the balcony walk above and the stairs down one side.

vacant after the Oakland Hills fire, and it was available partly because of the difficulties it presented: narrow, steep, irregular in form, close to adjoining houses, with a narrow southern exposure. These conditions demand an aggressive approach to the gathering of light.

As an artist, Mackota understood the importance of good light in every room, and he was excited about the potential for innovative solutions to the difficult problems of preserving privacy while admitting light on all sides of the building. He gave us very few design constraints, hoping for a home that would be adventurous and that would take advantage of its dramatic site.

The lot he purchased slopes steeply down to the south, open to both views and sunlight; but it is narrow, limiting the building's width on the southern face. The city requires a setback from side lot lines of only 5 ft. On narrow sites such as this, it is very likely that houses will be built right to this line. Here, the western side of the site has light and views blocked by another house just a few feet from property line. The lot to the east, though vacant during the design process, limited design freedom because of the prospect of a building that could be just 11 ft. away.

There was little flexibility in locating the building on this site; the 20-ft. street setback, the need to suspend the driveway and garage above the slope, and the desire to take advantage of the morning sun by placing the patio on the street side determined the garage location. The goal of maximizing southern exposure and the economically driven desire to minimize the footprint (foundation and roof are expensive building elements) gave shape to the remainder of the building. The resulting form is a tall, narrow building with a roofline that follows the slope and then tilts down to protect the front entry and garage doors. The side walls follow the property lines, resulting in a slightly skewed plan, with a cutout patio area to the northeast.

*Use shading devices to control
the amount of light and heat
that enters the house.*

LIGHT AS AN ORGANIZING FORCE

Given this rough envelope, the real design challenges lay, first, in placing rooms to take advantage of light and views; second, in bringing light into the rooms creatively and then providing enough shade to temper the light; and, third, in using the windows, skylights, and shade devices as major design elements to enliven the form. Rather than spreading across the site, this house is composed of rooms that stack vertically, which requires that most of the traffic flow take place on a staircase—a functional necessity that became the core idea for the organization of the house.

THE FLOW THROUGH ROOMS suggests that circulation should move along the edge of common spaces. To accomplish that, the staircase is placed at the center of the house and spirals down through five different levels at the edge of common areas on each floor. A large skylight above the stairwell spills light down its center, from the peak of the roof down to the lowest floor, brightening the middle of the house at each level and bathing the staircase in light. As you move down the open stairs, you move along the edge of the common spaces and overlook the spaces below. As a result, all the rooms feel strongly interconnected, yet each is defined by having its own level.

The kitchen, living room, and dining room are all located on the south side to capitalize on the views, the light, and the freedom from privacy concerns. High ceilings follow the roofline up to the central skylight, and windows are oversize to maximize light. The resulting rooms are generous and bright, with the feel of a warehouse or loft building—a quality that is accentuated by the metal windows in large-grid patterns. In the Bay Area, southern light brings the need for summer shade; this is provided by deep overhanging eaves at the kitchen and living room and by an exterior roll-down shade cloth screen (which allows a filtered view) at the dining area.

As the stairs continue down to the bottom of the house, a set of exterior stairs, with a screen of horizontal boards, filters the light to the reading/play space and bedrooms on the lower level. The same strategy is used at the entry deck and patio as well as outside the lower-floor bathroom, where the screen not only controls light but also offers a measure of privacy from the adjacent site.

Mezzanine/Entry Level

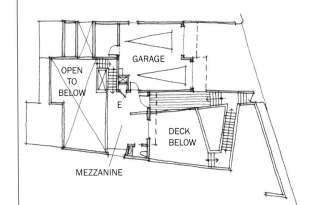

Main Level

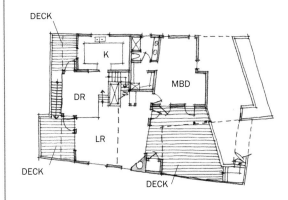

Lower Level

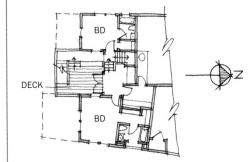

*Shape the house so that light can enter
every important room from at least
two sides to create balanced light.*

At the very bottom of this five-level home, a small alcove is carved into the space under the stairs—a perfect place for sitting and reading. The alcove looks through a large window, across a deck, to a view across the valley and offers both Refuge and Outlook.

With the dominant light in most rooms coming from the south, it is important to create balance with light from other directions. Light on two sides of every room is always our goal; we are constantly aware of the way in which the direction of light subtly influences our sense of space and our visual comfort. Rooms with windows on a single side tend to draw all our attention to that bright area; but then objects in front of the window are seen as dark silhouettes, lit only from behind. The effect is one of glare rather than illumination, and spaces away from the window tend to be lost in shadow. To counter this effect it is important to bring light from at least two directions. Light from above, light "borrowed" from another space through an interior window, and additional windows all work toward this end.

In this house, the dominant southern light demanded a balancing light source on the western side in two bedrooms, the kitchen, and the master bath. Each of these potential windows looked directly into the house next door. Curtains or shades might have provided a solution to the privacy problem, but they would also reduce the light available and would not fit comfortably with the clean lines of the house. Installing sandblasted glass at all windows with privacy issues solved the problem; soft light is abundant and, with window hinging carefully planned, privacy is complete even when the windows are open.

LIGHTING THE WAY

Light plays an important role in our language; symbolically we use "the light at the end of the tunnel" to describe arrival or completion, we say, "I see the light" to express understanding, and we talk of knowledge as enlightenment. We have developed these expressions because of the powerful impact light has on our life experience: It can lead us through a series of spaces, mark transitions, and call our attention to special places.

In the Mackota house, the play of light and shadow is used to guide visitors to the entry and to enhance the sense of transition from

street to house. Viewing the building from the road, we see that the windows and front door are tucked under deep eaves, but a window placed high in a large chimney serves as a beacon marking the house (and simultaneously admits light to a small bathroom below). From this vantage point, the entry deck floats above the courtyard below, its cantilevered entry roof offering shade and weather protection.

Where roof forms overlap at the entry, an upper skylight bounces light off the roof just above the front door, establishing it as the point of entry. In the daytime, visitors arriving on this deck pass into the house's shaded "umbrella" from the bright outdoor light, lead forward by the skylight. And after dark, the lighted passage and the windows of the mezzanine room offer a welcoming glow. A screen of horizontal wood members marks progress toward the door with a blending of light and shade, a play on the whole entry process. Once through the front door, the skylight over the stairwell is just ahead,

Sandblasted glass admits a soft glow of light and completely screens the view of the neighboring house, even with windows open.

A LIGHT TOUCH
WITH MATERIALS

The sense of lightness in a home is created not only by the amount of light that is brought in but also by the materials that are selected and the details of walls, handrails, windows, and doors. Each building style has a characteristic approach to the way in which light is admitted, the use of shadow, and the strength of the sense of enclosure. Early stone buildings were limited to small windows that could be spanned by a stone lintel. Because stone walls were thick, windows were deep set; thus, to increase light to the interior, jambs were splayed to reflect a soft light around the edge of the opening and reduce glare. The spaces in such buildings are cool, shadowy, protected, and quiet. In and out are strongly separated.

Over time, new technology led to stronger and lighter materials that made it possible to create walls with greater amounts of openness. The development of light wood and steel framing strategies allowed designers to place windows and doors almost anywhere in the building. The thin walls reduced the sense of transition from inside to out, and improvements in methods for producing and bonding large sheets of glass made very large openings possible. The modernist style capitalized on these developments with long horizontal bands

Materials in this contemporary home were selected for the ways in which they play with light. The aluminum handrail support and window frames were chosen for their ability to reflect light and dissolve the sense of structure. Pale and glossy wood floors bounce light up into the room, and white walls ensure brightness throughout.

of glass, suggesting a minimal structure supporting roofs floating above open plan spaces. The buildings feel light, airy, exposed, and strongly connected to the outdoors.

illuminating the stairway and promising more to come. Artificial lights installed in the skylight area ensure light from the same location at all times of day and night.

Perhaps the most exciting experience in this home is winding down the stairwell under the large ridge skylight that crowns the roof (see the photo on the facing page). The materials of the staircase are deliberately light and reflective. Rails are transparent to allow light through; and the central well spirals down through floors at five levels.

When windows or skylights are located on more than one side of a room, the space becomes filled with light, eliminating harsh shadows and reducing glare. The skylight here is installed flush with the walls below, allowing a wash of light down the wall surfaces.

Designing with Light

The experience of natural light in the home is so important that it affects the way a home is located on its site, the shape given to the building, the placement of each room, and the ways its skin is penetrated to admit light. Looking at homes from opposite sides of the country, we have seen the essential role that windows play in creating character and defining style. And by looking at details from a wide variety of homes, we have seen the importance of the openings in walls or ceilings in creating wonderful places within the home—walls washed with light or window bays or sunny pools. By capturing light and using it carefully to define form, to lead us through space, to reveal and conceal, we enliven our homes and our lives.

A house will feel comfortable only when all its parts—wings, roofs, walls, and openings—are in good proportion to each other and make up a balanced whole.

PARTS IN PROPORTION

The good proportions of this room begin with its generous height to width ratio and continue with the harmonious relationships between the beams, rafters, and ceiling boards.

YOU CAN PROBABLY REMEMBER SEEING A BUILDING that instinctively felt right. The various parts all seemed to fit together in a harmonious and comfortable way, each part apparently in the right place and in the right relationship to the whole. At the other extreme, you can probably remember seeing a building that felt somehow awkward—either unbalanced or confusing, with its parts appearing to be neither the right shape or size nor in the right place. These feelings are intuitive, but nonetheless solid and real. They come from our innate sense of proportion, from a feeling that the parts of an object need to relate well to each other.

Architects and builders throughout history have tried to create buildings that embody good proportion. Some architectural theorists—such as Vitruvius (first century B.C.) and Palladio (1508–1580)—tried to define good proportion by means of numerical rules: "The length of a room should equal 1½ times its width" or "the height of a room should be equal to its width." But while these numerical rules can be very helpful as guidelines, they are only a part of the story, since buildings with no strict rectangular geometry—composed of either varied angles or soft curves—often have very pleasing proportions as well.

The carefully coordinated subdivision of this wall into doors and fixed and operable windows gives the whole room a good sense of proportion.

129

This stone shed has a palpable sense of proportion. The individual stones roughly reflect the shape of the building and are echoed in the individual corrugated shingles of the roof.

PROPORTION IN NATURE
Virtually any fragment of nature, like this cutting from a back-yard bush, can serve to demonstrate the organizational properties of axis, balance, variety in unity, specialization, and similar form. These properties are at the heart of what we term good proportion.

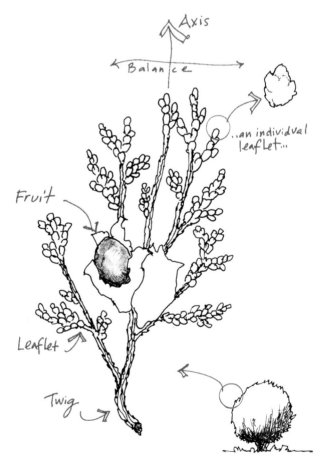

PROPORTION IN NATURE AND IN BUILDINGS

We get most of our sense of good proportion directly from nature. Virtually everything in nature seems to be "in proportion," whether or not it embodies strict geometry. The sizes and arrangements of the various body parts of any particular animal—from ant to fish, bird to cat—seem to be innately right, natural, and in proportion. Similarly the parts of a plant invariably appear to be in good proportion to each other, and to the whole.

A good way to relate proportion in nature to proportion in buildings is to compare the organization of a single example of flora (the common bush known as arborvitae) with the organization of a particularly well-formed house (in this case, a house that architect H. H. Harrison designed for his family in 1951). We'll look at six aspects of organic form that can help us create well-proportioned houses.

AXES OF GROWTH

The cutting has an obvious direction of growth, from the stem upward through the individual leaflets (see the drawing at left). Even though this growth responds to the local influences of neighboring branches and the availability of light and air, the resulting plant is clearly

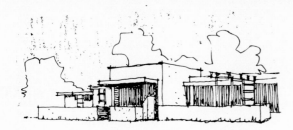

oriented along this main direction of growth. It has a starting point and orients toward a goal.

Similarly, the Harrison house grows along a line in plan that begins at the garage and entry, moves toward the front door, past the junction of the central hallway, and on into the living room, eventually leading to a dramatic central window and planter that opens out to the view beyond (see the drawing at right). As with the arborvitae, this axis is not necessarily a straight line, but it shifts subtly, responding to other influences. The house also has a vertical axis of growth, starting with a base of low walls and planters, followed by walls and windows, capped with sunshades and trellises. Our eye takes great pleasure in seeing the growth of an organism expressed in its final form—and we similarly appreciate the clarity of a house whose parts are arranged along a logical line, from entry to goal and from foundation up to roof.

BALANCE

The plant sprig is not rigidly symmetrical, but it is roughly balanced around its axis in both area and mass. Harrison's house shows the same balance around its axes, not strictly, but comfortably distributed around a center. In plan, balance around an axis can lead to an orderly and logical separation between different functions, such as between public and private spaces in a house. In elevation, balance around a vertical axis, with the highest portion in the center surrounded by lower supporting elements, leads to a feeling of graceful, natural stability.

SPECIAL PARTS

Like most organic objects, the arborvitae sprig is composed of distinct and specialized parts—stems, leaves, and fruits. Each is essential to the organism, and each takes on a unique form depending on its function—sturdy round stems for structure, flat leaves to absorb light, and spherical fruits to protect seeds.

The Harrison house grows from massive to delicate elements in the vertical direction, with the tall central volume balanced on all sides with successively lower elements.

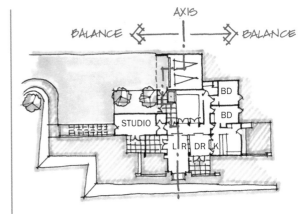

Balance around an axis is also embodied in the plan. It is arranged along a line that begins at the parking and entry, extends past the main hall circulation, through the living room, into the landscape beyond. The remaining parts of the house—office and bedrooms—are then balanced around this axis.

HUMAN-SIZE ROOMS

How big should a room be? Can it be too small—or too big? The greatest tool the designer has in this regard is the human body itself. A room will have "human scale" if it can be related to the size of the human body. If the smallest room does not incorporate circulation space at least the width of a human being (including swinging arms), it will be too small. If the largest rooms cannot be described and envisioned in terms of multiples of human height and width, it will probably feel too large.

Regardless of the merits of the decimal system, the English inch, foot, and yard all have the virtue of being immediately related to our bodies, and therefore easy to envision. Other human-based dimensional systems for sizing houses include the Malaysian finger–hand–arm system, the Japanese tatami mat, and Le Corbusier's modular system.

A traditional Malaysian house is built around a human-centered measurement system. The smallest dimensions are multiples of finger widths, followed by the widths of a closed hand, open hand, or two open hands. At the upper scale, the body and two extended arms allow the system to extend up to around 6 ft. in length.

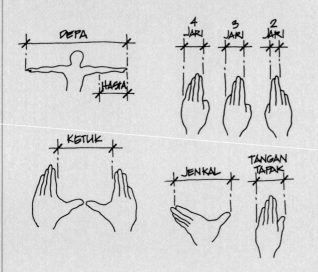

Malaysian House Measurements

Japanese House Measurements

3-MAT ROOM 3-MAT ROOM 4½-MAT ROOM 4½-MAT ROOM

6-MAT ROOM   8-MAT ROOM   10-MAT ROOM   12-MAT ROOM

The traditional Japanese house is planned around multiples of the tatami mat, roughly 3 ft. by 6 ft. (about the size of a single person's sleeping space). This unit of mat can be assembled to form 3-, 4½- 6-, 8-, 10-, or 12-mat rooms. This system has the virtue of producing rooms that are automatically human scaled, and well proportioned. The rooms have similar shapes (not identical), but can have many sizes.

Le Corbusier invented a system of building dimensions rooted both in the mathematics of harmonic progression and in the postural dimensions of the human body. The height of any building element would, for example, correspond to one of the following: a low bench (27 cm high), chair (27 cm + 16 cm = 43 cm high), writing table (27 cm + 16 cm + 27 cm = 70 cm high), workbench (27 cm + 16 cm + 27 cm + 16 cm = 66 cm high), and so on, up through low ledge, high ledge, man's height, to man's height plus raised arm. Thus his building elements fit natural human postures and scale.

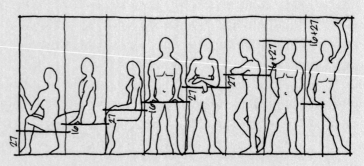

Le Corbusier's House Measurements

The Harrison house also clearly expresses its special parts—indoor rooms, outdoor rooms, circulation spaces, structural walls, and columns. In architecture, we sense proportion both in structural terms (the columns need to be thick enough to hold up the beams) and in functional terms (the halls have to be wide enough to serve the various rooms). The clear expression of the specialized parts of a house enables us to read the building and to understand how the building works. In practical terms, this means shaping indoor and outdoor rooms simply so that they can be felt as whole, enclosing spaces. It means giving structural posts and bearing walls ample dimensions so that they can not only support their loads but also look strong enough to support them. And it means giving circulation spaces, such as entries and halls, special identities—perhaps unique ceiling or floor treatments—to express their transitional functions.

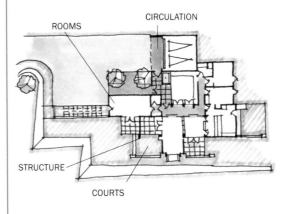

The architect clarified the specialized parts of the plan—circulation space, rooms and courts, and structural posts—to make the organization and structure of the house more visible.

The feeling of expansiveness of this great room is emphasized by the surrounding spaces of more modest size.

VARIETY IN SIZE

The leaves of a single tree come in a wide range of sizes, depending on their age and exposure to nutrients, sun, and stress. The Harrison house similarly has a large range of room sizes (both indoors and out) from the garage and central courtyard, through the individual bedrooms, down to the bathrooms.

This variety helps create a sense of comfort in the building. To make a house feel large and spacious, it's not enough simply to make everything bigger than normal. The resulting feeling of spaciousness will soon wear off, because there will be no adjacent medium and small spaces for comparison. We perceive sizes of objects in terms of relationships—"bigger than that, but smaller than that other one." The best way to make an object feel large, is to make it larger than the surrounding objects. This is why the concept of a great room in a house is so powerful. Selecting a single room in the house—usually the living/dining/cooking commons, but sometimes the family room—to have the largest area and highest ceiling of any other room makes it unique. The expansiveness of this one room can then be felt in contrast to the more modest ones.

UNITY OF SHAPE

Although the leaves of a tree vary widely in size, orientation, and details, it's clear that each has the same basic shape. Nature displays variety in unity. Similarly, a well-proportioned house contains rooms of different sizes, but of roughly the same shape.

The Harrison house has a number of indoor and outdoor rooms that vary widely in size and orientation, yet each has basically the same shape—a chubby rectangle. A building that has many sizes of similarly shaped rooms feels nicely

VARIETY IN UNITY

One of the reasons the Harrison house seems so well proportioned is that the many sizes of rooms and courtyards are unified by being approximately the same shape. In this house, the shape is a rough rectangle, slightly longer than it is wide.

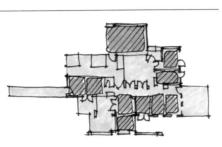

proportioned. The combination of a deep underlying unity and a seemingly infinite variety (what can be thought of as "texture") is a source of great aesthetic pleasure, whether it is found in nature, art, or architecture.

THE FORM OF THE WHOLE
EQUALS THE FORM OF THE PARTS

In nature, the overall shape emerges directly out of the shape of the elements. The shape of a bush's individual leaflet—a pointed oval—is repeated in the shape of the next larger branchlet, up to the branch, and up to the overall shape of the whole plant (see the drawing on p. 130).

Similarly, in a well-proportioned house, the shape of the whole will emerge naturally and directly out of the shapes of its individual parts. Forcing the various rooms and circulation spaces into a predetermined exterior shape, one that does not grow effortlessly out of the assembly of parts, will produce awkward proportions—if not on the exterior, then certainly on the interior.

FORM OF WHOLE = FORM OF PARTS *Although we don't expect a house of brick to look literally like a brick, the overall form of a well-proportioned house will emerge naturally from the forms of its various parts. In the Harrison house, the shape of the columns and the smaller spaces is similar to the shape of the larger rooms and to the larger groups of rooms, all leading naturally to the overall form of the house.*

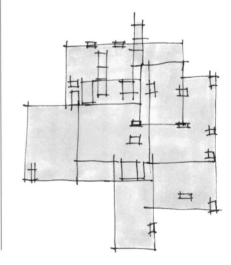

The same barnlike shape and proportion appear again and again, but in a rich variety of sizes and orientations.

THE POTATO-SHAPED ROOM

Using roughly similar shapes for the rooms gives unity to a house plan. But what *is* the shape of a well-proportioned room? We tell our students (and remind ourselves!) that rooms should be shaped more like a potato than a carrot—relatively compact and oblong not long and skinny. Generally, a room should be a little longer than wide, but not by much. This shape is flexible, naturally holding a single social gathering as well as two smaller ones. When we begin a design, we sketch rooms as fuzzy tuber-shaped blobs.

Palladio, the great sixteenth-century Italian architect, specified precise room proportions derived from the musical harmonies produced by specific lengths of vibrating strings or pipes full of oscillating air. But he also admitted that these ideal proportions could be modified as needed to fit the rooms into their places in the building. In effect, he advised that a room never be narrower than half its length and that the height never be less than the width. This produces rooms that are compact and chubby in volume—much like a potato.

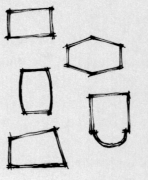

Rooms don't need to be crisp rectangles—they can be irregular with straight wall sections, or rounded. But generally they should be compact, oblong, and not too skinny.

Balance around a central axis, and the visible structural beams and rafters, combine to create a strong sense of proportion.

WORKING WITH THE PATTERN

A house needs to feel well proportioned, combining the variety of particular needs with an overall sense of stability and order. Rather than being a patchwork of disconnected elements, it should have the same fitness of form as a living organism.

- *Organize the house along lines of movement and growth,* both in plan and in elevation. One line, or axis, normally starts at the main entrance, branching out toward the sun and views, away from the street and its noise. Another begins at the ground and grows up toward the sky.

- *Balance the area and mass of the house* around these lines of growth. Let the plan grow outward on both sides of the main axis toward privacy and sun. And place the highest part of the house in the center, surrounded by lower supporting parts of the building.

- *Give the house visibly specialized parts:* solid structural elements that can be seen supporting the building, generously shaped rooms to contain activities, and distinctive circulation paths to conduct movement and flow through the house.

The blocky forms of the large elements of this house in the Pacific Northwest follow directly from the similar forms of the individual concrete blocks, windows, wooden walls, and roof beams.

◢ *Create a rich variety of room sizes and orientations*, always including human scale in the circulation, structure, trim, and openings.

◢ *Unify the rooms with a similar shape*, typically compact in plan and chubby in volume.

◢ *Let the overall form of the house grow naturally* out of the forms of its various parts, rather than being superimposed from outside. In this sense the form of the house equals the form of its parts.

This pattern does not dictate the geometry or style of the design. It will help a strictly symmetrical Neoclassical house have satisfying proportions, just as it will a Craftsman cottage. On the other hand, a sinuously organic design that does not embody good proportions could easily be ill proportioned. The houses presented for this pattern illustrate a wide range of styles, but each shows the principles of good proportion at work.

Good balance and proportion doesn't demand symmetry. This house achieves its harmony through repeated use of similarly shaped forms assembled into a roughly balanced whole.

MAIN FLOOR *The chunky, compact proportions of the rooms that make up the plan are extended upward into the vertical dimension to produce the similarly chunky and compact exteriors.*

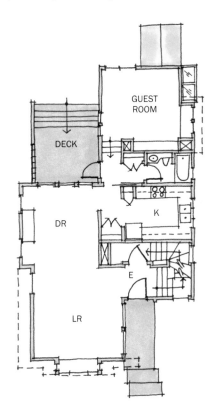

A WELL-ORDERED CLUSTER OF FORMS

Jeffrey Limerick's house in Boulder, Colorado, steps back from the street and presents a well-orchestrated assembly of building blocks, roof forms, and textures in the dignified manner of many traditional Boulder homes.

The house is an example of informal, asymmetric balance and proportion. The two main front masses of the house remain in balance because they each have a center—a large, high window centered under a symmetrical portion of roof. They share similar materials, colors, and textures. They share one roof surface and are, therefore, actually part of a larger entity.

This can be better understood from a side view of the house, which shows overall form as an assembly of similar gable-roofed volumes, intersecting at right angles, stepping down from the tallest to the lowest front window bay on the street (see the photo on the facing page).

In terms of details, the protruding roof beams nicely divide the large building blocks into two side aisles and a middle bay and invite us to see the parts that make up the whole. The vertical battens that cover the lines of nails in the wall studs behind further subdivide the wall into rich, vigorous surfaces with a good sense of scale. Vertical scale is achieved by the use of a base of lighter stained plywood, the trellises, and the trim at the horizontal plywood joints.

Good proportions on the outside grow directly out of the plan. Each of the rooms, both inside and out, has a fat rectangular shape. The rooms are then organized to form two larger halves, each shifted relative to each other to form the entry in the front and the deck in the back. The resulting plan, and the resulting volume of the house, is composed of the same bulky rectangular proportions. This unity of shape is a hallmark of good proportion.

The rooms and volumes of the Limerick house are packed together in a relaxed, informal manner. The next house we'll look at, on the other hand, is a distillation of space to its most essential elements, expressed in a pure, clean geometry. Yet the principles of proportion are the same.

Let the overall form of the house grow naturally out of the forms of its various parts. The form of the house equals the form of its parts.

From the largest volumes down to the smallest elements, the house has good proportions. The chunky building blocks are varied in size and orientation but are similar in shape. Likewise, the linear elements of trim and trellis contribute a lot of variety to the surface but also tend to unify the entire skin of the building.

Elegant Proportions, from Site to Trim

THE DOYLE RESIDENCE IN NORTHERN CALIFORNIA, is a stage for outdoor living in a space formed by retaining walls, an orchard, and the surrounding buildings. Given the generally mild weather in the Napa Valley, the architect conceived of the entire site as outdoor living space, supported by buildings that provide shelter during the infrequent rains or cold nights. But what elevates this house to a work of art is its embodiment of good proportion at all levels, from the site plan down to the textures of the building materials.

SHAPING THE SITE

The house is sited on a gently sloping, open landscape, without indigenous trees or other features to provide anchors. The architect, Eric Haesloop of Turnbull Griffin Haesloop, began by creating parallel upper and lower retaining walls to form a habitable flat building and living site and then outfitted it with the support structures of garage, house, study, pool, and orchard. The upper retaining wall with its accompanying pool was shaped to follow a slight indentation in the hill, thereby creating a unique feature within the otherwise rectilinear geometry. As a result, the pool is quite visible from within the house (and gets ample direct sun).

The long, thin main house runs perpendicular between the two retaining walls, bisecting the flat area to create balanced and strongly defined rectangular courts on either side—the entry court defined by a detached garage and the living court completed by a detached study, pool, and orchard. The long axis of the main house, the resulting near-symmetry of the building site, and the variety of similarly shaped rectangular spaces and building volumes are the foundations of the site plan's good proportions.

At every level from outside to in this California house offers the deep peace that can come with a superbly well-ordered composition, a beautifully proportioned building.

A carefully proportioned level yard for outdoor living is carved out of the sloping landscape and outfitted with supporting buildings, pool, and plantings.

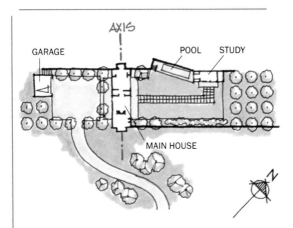

SITE PLAN *Around an axis through the length of the main building, the outdoor space and building mass to the left roughly balances the outdoor space and building mass to the right. The outdoor spaces and individual rooms are of widely varying sizes, but all are similarly shaped rectangles, bringing the entire site into careful proportion.*

From the entry gate, the house greets us with a massive bay window of elegant proportions. It announces a house designed with great care and confident restraint.

The proportions of the entry are carefully refined, with the details of columns, windows, and doors concentrated at the center and surrounded by expanses of unbroken wall and roof surface.

A MEASURED ARRIVAL

The sense of proportion is first encountered as you arrive by car. Pausing at the gate, you're greeted by a huge bay window (the dining area off the kitchen) that overlooks the driveway and the fields beyond. It forms a kind of welcoming lantern for the arriving visitor. The bay window is subdivided into smaller panes, creating top, middle, and bottom portions and left, middle, and right thirds—that is, into centers with balancing elements. The subsequent subdivision of these panes into vertical halves adds further interest and texture.

Incidentally, because you are approaching from *below* the house, you are not yet able to look into the east private yard (see the photo on p. 141), a view that must wait until you've passed through the main house. This preserves the yard's privacy yet allows residents in the yard to see who is coming, an example of the pattern REFUGE AND OUTLOOK.

From the entry court, the main house presents a dignified face. The six white porch columns define five square-shaped voids, with the middle one reserved for the front door (see the photo below). This squareness is echoed in the shape of the door and window frames, which are again subdivided into nicely proportioned (double square) panes of glass. These various elements are so uncluttered that we are able to focus on their proportions and appreciate the care with which they were composed.

Note, for example, how the roof vents are clustered together to minimize their disturbance of the broad, regularly patterned roof surface. And how the windows and doors are gathered under the porch roof to concentrate the detail in the center and permit plain unbroken wall surfaces at each end. Under the porch at the front door, the simplicity of walls, deck, and even light fixtures continues; but the exposed ceiling begins to give a hint of the proportional richness that awaits inside.

A BALANCED INTERIOR

Looking at the floor plan of the main house, you can see that the house has two axes, or lines, of development. The first stretches from the most public (front dining room bay window) to the most private (the shower at the back of the master bedroom), around which the house is symmetrical on both sides. The second runs from the entry at the front porch, alongside the boxlike powder room/guest closet and laundry, through to the back porch doors. This axis is roughly balanced by the commons and the private areas, each of which is further

MAIN HOUSE PLAN *The plan of the main house is an elegant example of proportionality, showing balance around two axes, specialized boxes of function, and the reuse of similar shapes at a variety of scales.*

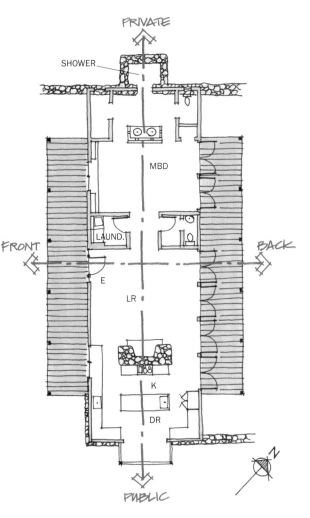

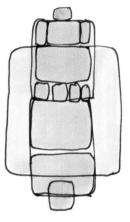

Room size varies greatly, but all rooms have roughly the same potato shape.

subdivided by more boxes—the living room from the kitchen/dining area by the fireplace; the master bedroom from the master bath by closet, toilet, and sink boxes. An echo of this is seen in the detached study, in which the space is broken down into a living space in the middle surrounded by a bath to the left and a mechanical room to the right. This overall attention to balance gives the house a sense of calm stability and strength, similar to the feeling of a graceful, mature tree.

The plan also displays a range of sizes of rectangles, from big rooms to small closets, each roughly the same chubby shape (see the drawing at left). In these ways, the geometry of the building is full of both variety and order, the same quality that we see in nature, even though the house is composed of straight lines and right angles rather than organically curving lines.

STRUCTURAL RHYTHM

The interior volume of the rooms follows directly from the overall shape of the building—just as the stone fireplace box is itself constructed to reflect this overall shape, with its shoulders sloped in at the same angle as the roof. At an even smaller level, the rocks are roughly the same shape as the firebox that they form. These are all examples of the same form being used again and again at different scales. Most striking is the exposed roof framing, which offers one of the most powerful sources of good proportion in this house. Infrequent big beams, supporting more frequent smaller joists, topped by very thin and small purlins at the highest frequency creates a visible rhythm of structure, the same rhythm that underlies the structure of a tree.

The detached study has the same interior proportions as the main house, only at a smaller scale (see the photo on p. 128). The exposed roof framing shows how division, subdivision, and sub-subdivision can create a strong sense of good proportion, bringing the rhythms of construction down to human scale. The main roof beams first divide the volume into a middle and two edges. Then the rafters, running perpendicular to the beams, subdivide the length of the room into person-wide sections. Finally, purlins, running perpendicular to the rafters, cut the space between rafters into hand-size sections.

Good proportion informs the shapes of the rooms, the firebox, and most of all the rhythm of the exposed roof framing. A spray of kicker posts sprouting from the top of the fireplace helps reduce the span on the roof beams and shapes the ceilings of both the living room and the kitchen.

The small central passageway that leads to the bedroom zone is topped with a dramatic skylight, emphasizing the transition between the public and private areas of the house.

USING LIGHT TO EMPHASIZE PROPORTION

While this house is a wonderful example of Parts in Proportion, it could also be used to illustrate many other patterns, such as COMPOSING WITH MATERIALS, REFUGE AND OVERLOOK, and especially CAPTURING LIGHT. Part of the elegance of this house stems from the way light is used to reinforce the proportions of the building. At the very center of the house, over the passageway connecting the living room and bedroom, a skylight brings light down into the heart of the commons as a momentous marker of the separation between the zones of the building.

CAPTURING LIGHT *Light is introduced dramatically at the central hallway and at the two ends, emphasizing the proportions of the major spaces and the transitions that define them.*

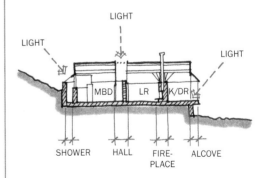

The dining room bay simultaneously works as a light gatherer, overlook, and definer of the overall proportions of the kitchen.

The dining room bay, which greets visitors as they drive up to the house, acts as a south-facing light gatherer for the entire kitchen, helping define it as an entity within the house and as an important "end" of the house. This bay window also works as an outlook over the landscape spread out below, giving it the feel of the wheel room of a great ship.

In contrast, at the opposite end of the house a shower room is dug into the hill on the north. The uniqueness of this cavelike room is also emphasized by light, but this time it comes into the space from above, falling on the stone of the enclosing retaining wall. A hint of this light is visible from the master bedroom and starts to come into full view as you round the edge of the massive headboard/room divider (see the photos on the facing page).

The sensuality of this space derives in part from the luxuriousness of the smooth 1-in.-square blue tile mosaic floor in contrast with the rough rawness of the surrounding rock walls (COMPOSING WITH MATERIALS). And the secure solidness of the windowless rock wall surround contrasts with the startling openness of the roof skylight (REFUGE AND OUTLOOK).

The house invites and supports use of the outdoors. It incorporates a geometry that leads us from shelter and security, through in-between spaces that prepare us for the outdoors, to well-formed outdoor rooms that establish a frame for our activities.

From the bedroom, a triangle of light above the headboard hints at a space beyond. As you go around the massive divider, the space is revealed as the master shower, dug into the hill at the northern end of the building.

A House That Grows into Its Gardens

IN CONTRAST TO THE CLASSIC, JEWEL-LIKE PRECISION of the Doyle house, we end our discussion of proportion with a house that has the order of a western mining town, built over time by many individual owners—each with a different purpose and budget—but unified by a single building type.

This Colorado home is a large residence composed of many smaller elements, almost all of them rectangular in plan, which are repeated, stretched, and twisted and then linked together into various wings that reach out into space for light, air, and visual contact with the surrounding gardens and natural landscape. Each of these elements begins with a simple gable roof, which is then either pitched up slightly in one direction, joined by an attached shed roof, or embellished with an attached flat trellis. But because the various parts are similarly shaped, the sprawling building gains a sense of wholeness and order. Repeating the same proportions in the roof form in different ways (using a range of materials, raising one room up into a tower) ties the building together but allows variety. It is the kind of variety you see in a building or town that has grown over time, the various parts adapting to different historical needs and conditions.

A FARM FOR LIVING

Like farm buildings, the elements are set out just as needed, informally, with an eye toward each one's special function and place in the whole. The owner wanted the feel of midwestern agriculture buildings arranged artfully in the landscape to create garden opportunities, and she started out wanting a rather conservative house. But working with the architect, Scott Lindenau, she began to enjoy the process of exploration and design, the evolution of ideas. Together they took the familiar forms of farm buildings and started to transform them into the spaces needed for both the house and the various gardens in a fresh and sometimes playful manner.

The house has an organic brand of proportionality. It grew by the assembly of many different but related volumes, all balanced around the view to the pond.

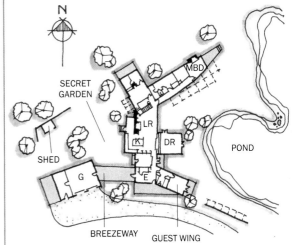

SITE PLAN *The plan of the house reaches out into the landscape to form distinct garden landscapes—the pond to the east, the secret garden to the west, and a smaller protected garden to the north.*

The simple rural forms of the house are arranged informally but always shaping well-proportioned outdoor spaces.

Create a rich variety of room sizes and orientations, always including human scale in the circulation, structure, trim, and openings.

The site, near Aspen, Colorado, is unusual for the area in that it is flat. And common to that area, it is surrounded by good views. The site plan began with one of the owner's main requests—a pond, large enough to support fish and to attract birds and elk. The major interior spaces of the house all share a view of the pond.

The informal flavor of the house is evident at the main entry on the south side (compare it to the more formal entry of the Doyle house) where each simple gabled volume is altered in some way to generate variety. For example, an extensive lean-to has been added to the garage, creating the impression of a barn for cars. The main house, its garage on the left, and the attached guest wing on the right are all set at slight angles to each other, which creates a welcoming gesture at the front—as well as an unusual intersection between the entry porch roof and the attached guesthouse. Further playful notes include the porch columns that lean out from the building, and the ridge of guesthouse that rises slightly toward the east (as if to reach out and capture more morning light).

The occasional changes in materials (sheet-metal roofing to fiberglass) and color (natural wood siding and stained gray siding beyond) also contribute to the relaxed attitude. Yet in spite of all this variety, the house gives an initial impression of being well proportioned. And this is because it incorporates the characteristics of the underlying kind of proportion that we find in nature—a rich variety constrained by basic rules, balance around axes, an overall form that grows naturally out of the assembly of the parts, and textures that are at human scale.

With its consistently twisted and angled forms, the entry gives the impression of a relaxed, informal, even playful house, but one that is well proportioned.

The breezeway, viewed from the house back toward the garage with the secret garden on the right, demonstrates the beauty of good proportion. The roof framing and the layout of the glazed walls show nested rhythms of similar shapes with a great variety of sizes, all balanced around the main center line and around each of the structural bays.

The breezeway not only connects garage and house but also helps form the boundary of the secret garden and offers a welcome opportunity to enjoy it in passing.

THE BREEZEWAY CONNECTION

The garage is linked to the house by a glazed breezeway, which constitutes one of the secret garden's defining boundaries, helping shape it as an outdoor room rather than just as an open space. This is a great example of the pattern CREATING ROOMS, INSIDE AND OUT. It's also a good example of the pattern THE FLOW THROUGH ROOMS, working at the scale of the whole site, showing how powerful circulation can be in animating the space it serves.

This breezeway is about 10 ft. wide, big enough to serve not only as a passage but also as a greenhouse. The framing is carefully laid out to create a primary rhythm of major roof beams set on concrete exterior posts (formed with sections of galvanized steel storm drain) placed approximately 8 ft. on center. Above this structure, the secondary rhythm of roof rafters marches down the breezeway set at about 2 ft. on center. Finally, the roofing purlins form the third overlaid rhythm. The effect of all this care in framing proportions is the feeling of being inside an exquisitely delicate structure, full of order and delight.

IN SCALE

It's a common mistake to think that being in proportion means being small. Rather, it means being in scale, in making either a large or modest gesture, but doing it in a manner that lets us see the scale of our bodies embedded in its structure. The porch off the guest wing of this house is a good example of being in scale.

While the covered porch is large and high, the siding texture of the wall is defined by the wooden battens, spaced at hand-span distance from each other—8 in. or 9 in. The big diagonal roof brackets end well above head height, but begin down at waist level, where we can lean against them. The wall is big but is brought back into scale by an upper window (to let light down into the guest room), which plays a trick with our eye: If that window indicates a second story, then the building is unusually low! And the roof, which has been gradually sneaking up in height all along the length of this wing, finally breaks out in a wonderful gable-end extension to create a very generous covered space below. This roof itself is composed of familiar, comfortably sized rafters and purlins, moving down to the 3-in. scale of the corrugations of the plastic roofing.

The large size of the guest-wing porch is tempered by the human scale of the wall batten spacing, the low starting point of the diagonal roof braces, the upper window, and the visibility of the roof framing elements.

BRINGING IT HOME

A Well-Proportioned House

A house needs to embody compositional order, a set of rules that governs its geometry and proportions. Our deepest aesthetic sensibilities originate from the compositional order in nature, and we can apply nature's rules to our analysis of beautiful houses. Both geometrical crystalline forms and sinuous organic ones can possess good proportion and order, and this is equally true of both classically formal houses—like the Doyle house—and those that grow more contextually and informally—like the Colorado residence.

Regardless of its style, a well-proportioned and ordered house is roughly balanced around lines of growth or development—from the ground up to the sky, from the public front through to the most private back. Its similarly shaped parts are repeated again and again in different sizes and variations. It expresses its specialized parts (circulation, rooms, structure) clearly, helping us understand how they work. And the house is in scale: The people who live there can find their own physical dimensions reflected in the fabric of the surrounding building.

Restated themes are at the heart of good proportion: The rear elevation of the kitchen repeats the shape of the garage; the color of the upper deck reflects that of the rusty roofing; and the various angles are repeated in different forms.

A house and its site should be shaped so that the main flow of traffic moves along the edges of the common rooms, exposed to the activity within but not a part of it.

THE FLOW THROUGH ROOMS

Passing through a gateway, following a path, stepping onto a porch—these activities work together to create a smooth transition from the world outside to the comfort within this Ohio home.

ARRIVING AT, MOVING INTO, AND TRAVELING around a house is a completely different way of knowing a building than the more static feeling of simply being in a room. Rooms are designed to contain, to define space, to create settings for the activities that occur within them. As you travel through rooms—entering, leaving, passing along their edges—it is necessary to approach spaces with a unique awareness, paying attention to many things at once: where you are going, the rhythm of the movement, the spaces you are passing, the surface you are moving along.

CREATING ROOMS, OUTSIDE AND IN showed that the whole site can be thought of as being composed of rooms. The different opportunities (or challenges) presented by each new location—each room—must be bridged by some form of connecting space, and that space plays several important roles. It offers an introduction to the next space—*arrival*; it contains the movement as you travel from one spot to the next—*passage*; and it provides a space to adjust from one experience to another—*transition*.

To accomplish all these tasks effectively, the connecting space must become a real link, including enough of the qualities of

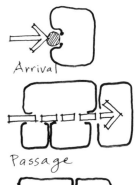

Arrival

Passage

Transition

Well-designed circulation passages are more than just a way to get from room to room. This hall encourages pausing; it offers a window seat with enough space to sit briefly, a chance to enjoy the view as you move past the windows, and a sunny spot to grow flowers. The play of stone textures and light creates an active feel that is different from the more tranquil and highly finished quality of the rooms beyond, while the finish of the windows and doors creates continuity between the spaces.

each of the rooms it joins to soften the edge between them and ease the transition. At the same time, the space must have enough of an identity of its own to allow a real pause—a moment to gather thoughts and belongings before moving on. This difference in the way rooms and passages are experienced presents real challenges in home design—often a single space will play both roles at different times—but it also creates some of the most rewarding and memorable experiences a house can offer.

WORKING WITH THE PATTERN

Houses vary. In small homes it's important to minimize the total area used by traffic flow (or circulation), whereas in large homes it may be more important to create spaces that celebrate the movement from room to room. In all homes, however, a few simple strategies can help create a graceful flow through rooms:

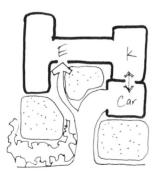

- *The flow through rooms begins at the street;* plan circulation outdoors as carefully as indoors.

- *Locate the main entry near the center of the house* it serves and link it directly with the major circulation routes.

- *Plan a car connection for both residents and guests;* allow for relatively short distances where heavy loads must be carried—from car to kitchen—and make the route to the entry clear to visitors.

- *Place rooms along a privacy gradient,* with the most public spaces near the entry and the most private more remote.

- *Borrow space from the edges of the more public rooms* to create *passages* that enliven the space but don't disrupt the activities taking place within.

- *Define each transition in a house* in a way that offers a moment's pause—a chance to leave the space you are in and contemplate the space you are about to enter.

- *Locate staircases so that they leave the main circulation route* and arrive in an upstairs hall in the midst of the rooms they serve.

- *Give circulation spaces a distinctive form;* define them with architectural elements: gates, changes in floor or wall material, overhead beams, different ceiling heights, columns or half-walls.

- *Make the most efficient use of space* and enliven circulation paths by giving them additional uses as libraries, galleries, and storage and display areas; offer short-term seating when it is possible.

Circulation paths can lead us to an understanding of the building and its outdoor spaces as a whole rather than as a series of parts. When the flow through rooms is smooth, the transition is gradual and the thresholds are marked, a house slowly unfolds, revealing more about itself as it is used. Too often the design of a house focuses almost exclusively on the quality of the rooms—the circulation routes are superimposed after the layout has been planned, fitted into left-over spaces, and squeezed into or between rooms. The results are long, dark corridors with no clear destinations, rooms disrupted by traffic through the middle of activity areas, and circuitous paths that consume too many square feet and construction dollars.

Privacy Gradient

Moving along Edges

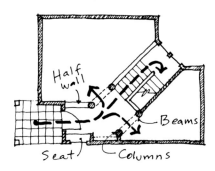

Central Circulation

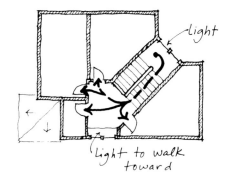

In this California house, the passage along the edge of the dining room connects the kitchen to the front entry and living room. Filled with light from the French doors that link the dining area to the terrace outside, its central location encourages informal use of the dining room for homework and coffee breaks and allows expansion of the table for special events.

Time spent moving around these poorly thought out pathways is devoted purely to "getting there" and does not enhance the experience of the house. Creating passages that really earn their keep in a home demands careful attention to organizing the whole as well as placing value on the processes of arrival, passage, and transition, which work together to funnel activity into and through the rooms of the house.

ARRIVAL:
AN INTRODUCTION TO HOME

As you approach your own house, there's usually some point at which you breathe a sigh of relief and feel—ahhhh, *home*. That point may be where you turn onto a tree-lined street, cross a bridge, or leave the paved road for a gravel drive. It may be at the garden gate or the step onto the front porch. A boundary has been crossed and suddenly you are on familiar ground, you have arrived. Usually, there is some significant change in the surroundings that accompanies that moment—a change in direction, different materials, passing under or through some kind of gateway. How satisfying the moment of arrival is, how welcoming the setting, depends on how effectively the transition from one space to another is defined.

Marking the entry with gates, changes in direction or level, a different texture of the ground-covering material, or a variation in the quality of light or color, smell or sound makes the experience memorable and makes each return more meaningful. These subtle boundary markers are stored in the mental file we create marked "home" or "Joe's house," and coming in contact with them opens the file and helps us prepare for being in that space. A home is made up of many arrivals. Arriving at the site, leaving the car, coming into an outdoor room, reaching the front door, entering a room, moving into a more private space are all important experiences that deserve special attention. Much of the character of a house is determined by the experience of coming and going at every scale.

THE CAR CONNECTION

Design of an entry begins at the street—it is the first exposure to the house and it's where lasting impressions are created. Because cars travel quickly and a driver's ability to see detail is limited, planning arrival at the street edge requires thinking at a different scale. For visitors, it is useful and reassuring to have an identifiable target in mind as they approach a home. "The only house with a red gate" is easier

The entry to the Limerick house is straightforward—a walk through the garden to a bright red front door sheltered by a trellis. But the care paid to each detail creates a warm welcome. The curving walk that leads to the door is colored in natural tones and includes a generous seating space just outside the door. The trellis creates the sense of protection at the entry, and the final step up to the landing establishes arrival.

In rainy Oregon, a covered walk to the entry is greatly valued. Here, the walkway travels along the edge of a generous outdoor room: a garden that introduces visitors to the house as they approach the front door.

to find than number 201, often hidden in the plantings. Gateways, fences, a colonnade of trees, a lamp post, are all ways to create identity and differentiate this house from all others.

Once the house is located, it is important both to provide a clear sense of how to approach the house (where to park the car, what door to walk toward) and to create boundaries that can be experienced from a car—for example, passage through a hedge or transition onto a different paving material. The breezeway at the Apter house by Thallon and Edrington, Architects (shown above) addresses these issues by providing a covered walkway between the front entry of the house and the garage. It features both a direct garage connection and a pedestrian gateway—a very visible gabled roof at an angle to the walk and the guest parking area—and it creates a clear edge between the zone of the car and the garden.

Residents and visitors typically arrive at a house by car—a pattern that doesn't reflect how people lived when most house forms evolved. Traditional homes typically had a well-marked front door, used by visitors and for formal occasions, and a back door, often opening onto a porch connecting the kitchen to the garden, used for daily coming and going. In many homes today, the garage has replaced the back door, and the front door is positioned as if most visitors would arrive by foot. The result is that residents arrive through a utilitarian garage and guests are puzzled about where to park their cars and unclear about how to enter. The car connection for both visitors and guests deserves as much attention as the front entry. One solution to this predicament is presented in "Park and Enter" on the facing page.

CREATING THE CAR CONNECTION
The pedestrian gateway, placed at an angle to the rest of the walk, defines the entry and offers a contained view into the large outdoor room to the south of the house.

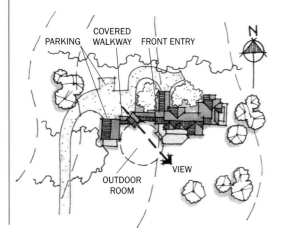

A WELCOMING MAIN ENTRY

A visible and appealing main entry both orients and welcomes. There are three critical design issues to consider: first, to make it intuitively clear where the main entrance is located; second, to define a route that feels natural and relatively direct; and, third, to create an exterior look that is one of the most memorable images of the building. At the

The front entry of this Oregon house by Jim Givens is a compressed introduction to a complex and delightful house (discussed in detail on p. 175). The entry is sheltered under a gable roof over a balcony overlook on the second floor and recessed into the building to create a real sense of protection. The Craftsman-style front door is set in a surround of glass, allowing a glimpse into the house.

PARK AND ENTER

Creating a well-planned car connection—an entrance that specifically addresses the need for a place to park the car but also recognizes the psychological need to experience a welcoming setting for arrival—is a critical design challenge in most homes. This connection can take many forms. One example is the graceful breezeway in the house by Huestis Tucker Architects shown below. The breezeway creates a weather-protected link between the garage and the family areas of the house and simultaneously connects the front yard to a sitting area in the side garden. The garage placed off to the side of the house, its doors discreetly turned away from the street, helps create a real outdoor room in the private rear garden; the breezeway then becomes the "front door" to that room.

front door, it's also important to address the practical concerns and to create real comfort (see "Focus on the Practical" on p. 167). Once the door is swung open, the house should reveal something subtle and unexpected: a view through the building, sunlight washing an interior wall, a pattern on the floor. And the main entry must tie to the circulation paths through the house, encouraging a natural movement along the intended route. Let's begin by looking at an excellent example of a large home with a relatively informal but masterful approach to circulation.

Going with the Flow

A long flagstone path leads from an arched entry gate to the front door, which is set deep within a broad arched opening that echoes the gate. The path is inviting, and the route is clear.

WHEN YOU ARRIVE AT THE DRIVEWAY to this Ohio residence, it is immediately apparent that the house stands a bit apart from its neighbors. In a world of straight driveways and manicured lawns, this home, by Centerbrook Architects, features a gently curved drive approaching a house half hidden among the trees.

At the end of the drive, a gravel court (the first outdoor room) circles a large tree, allowing cars an easy turnaround and providing a location for guest parking that is clear but informal (see the photo on p. 164). The garages discreetly turn their doors away from the street. The house remains hidden behind a tall courtyard wall with an inviting gate under a gentle arch. Entering that gate is like crossing a threshold, bringing the visitor into a generous landscaped room that is as much a part of the house as the kitchen or the living room—an excellent example of CREATING ROOMS, OUTSIDE AND IN.

With a swing of the gate, the world of the street, the car, and the neighborhood is left behind and a new realm of quiet is revealed. Ahead, a generous outdoor room acts as an entry court. The garage and the house shape the space on two sides in a kind of lazy L form, while the courtyard wall creates a boundary at the remaining edges. Off to one side is a smaller alcove of space filled with seating (a private edge off a common core), but the path from the gate leaves no question about how to approach the main entrance.

Another arch lies ahead above the porch containing the front door. In the daytime, this protected space is lit from above by high windows, while at night concealed lighting lets it glow like a lantern. The light draws visitors along the flagstone path across the courtyard, toward

The entry courtyard is enlivened by a series of small spaces at the edges. Here, a sitting area close to the house feels protected by the nearby walls but allows enjoyment of the expanse of space beyond.

A GENTLE APPROACH

The gently curved driveway contrasts with the straight approach to the neighboring houses.

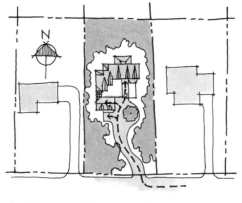

Garage opening faces away from the street.

Enclosure on two sides by the building and the high fence of the inner courtyard creates an outdoor room for cars—a spacious car court that allows for easy turns around the tree island as well as plenty of guest parking.

the front door, and the deep recess creates a comfortable room that offers protection and celebrates arrival. It is the number and variety of transitions that makes this arrival process so extraordinary. Textures change from gravel to loose-laid flagstone then to set stone, before finally becoming the polished wood of the entry hall: Each change becomes more refined, more interior.

MOVING AROUND INSIDE THE HOUSE

The outdoor entry room and then the generous front door lead into an interior central stair hall. Lit from above and overlooked by a bridge joining upstairs rooms, this space distributes its users in all directions: upstairs to the bedrooms, downstairs to the living room on one side, or along a unique "wave wall" toward the kitchen on the other (see the floor plan on p. 166). A coat closet and a small powder room are tucked to each side of the front door in blocks that form a deep pocket for the entry and screen the view of the living and dining rooms to each side from a casual caller.

Moving around this home is such an adventure that it is hard to think of it in terms of efficiency; yet the circulation here is laid out to minimize the amount of space devoted to halls and the amount of travel required to move around this rather large building. The central stairway effectively collects all the travel upstairs and uses a short hall in each direction to serve the four bedrooms and two bathrooms. The passages branching off to each side are short and enlivened by windows open to below. On the lower floor, the master bedroom suite opens just off the stairs. When the upstairs is not in use, all of the rooms used daily by the owners are close together.

The most dramatic passage in the house is an unusual wavy path that flows along the edge of the kitchen and the dining room and terminates at the foot of the stairs, linking all of the major rooms of the house (see the bottom photo on

Located at the crux of the house, the staircase features a bridge above that looks down into both the interior and exterior entry halls—an unusual passage between in and out.

p. 166). The shape of the wall invites motion, guiding the flow from the entry and the stairs past the dining table and the kitchen toward the den—an intimate sitting space that is concealed around a curve.

A SECOND ENTRY

A glazed breezeway provides a sheltered connection between the den and the garage (see the top photo on p. 166). A semiconditioned space, this passage is unheated but protected from harsh weather by the roof and side walls, and somewhat warmed by its connection to the house. With a strong visual connection to the garden, it is a space that really combines out and in. It meets all the practical needs associated with arriving home, offering protection from the weather, a gradual introduction to the change in temperature, and a place to remove wet boots or to keep sports equipment.

For visitors, the convenient guest parking in the car court, the invitation of the gate, and the visually clear route to the front door create a welcoming and easily understood arrival process. Owners arriving in the garage benefit from an equally well thought out sequence of events—a gradual transition from outside to inside through increasingly tempered spaces. And once indoors, everyone can enjoy the wave wall—a passage that captures the essence of The Flow through Rooms.

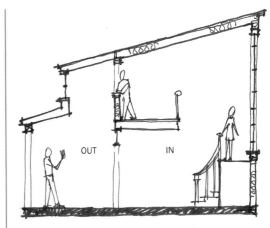

The entry room is a generous two-story space bisected by the front door, half inside and half out, and filled with light from both directions.

More like a greenhouse than a hall, the glassy breezeway linking the garage to the house creates a natural transition from being outdoors to arriving home.

A HOUSE WITH TWO ENTRIES

Visitors arrive at the gate and then follow the walk to the front entry in the midst of the common rooms. Residents park in the garage and enter through the breezeway, arriving close to the kitchen. The two entries are linked by the dramatic flow along the wave wall.

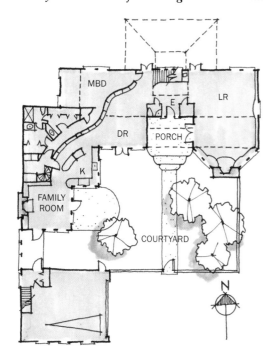

The wave wall offers a changing display to those who pass along its gentle curves. Connecting the entry to the kitchen, it keeps traffic flow at the edge of the dining room.

FOCUS ON THE PRACTICAL

When planning your own entry, picture graceful entrances you have experienced, tracking your route from outside in. Imagine the area immediately around the main entrance as a room, bisected by the front door. Consider the impact of the entrance on the floor plan, the way the common spaces and the staircase tend to be tied to it. Outside the door, create a sheltered place to wait out of the rain; a place to set down a package and fumble for your keys. Offer a place to sit and provide a shoe scraper or door mat. Fill the area with soft light from the side, not from above (which can create harsh shadows on the face). Then add personal touches: potted plants, a bright door, a polished knocker.

Once inside, consider the practical gestures that make coming home comforting. If you live in a cold climate, create an airlock—a small space between exterior doors and an interior door that prevents the wind from blowing into the house through an open door. Provide a place to put boots and shoes, and a place to sit while they are removed. Think about where to put keys, mail, umbrellas, hats, and coats. A mirror in the entry is useful both for last minute touch-ups and for arriving guests. Windows or a view port that allow residents to see arriving visitors increases security. In houses with small children, plan space for a stroller and other such paraphernalia.

At a garden or back entry, consider a mudroom with a link to traffic flow through the house. Plan the connection to the car, and provide a place to put down cumbersome loads. This can be a convenient place to store sports equipment and gardening supplies—and a place to wash and dry pets (fitted out with their own access door).

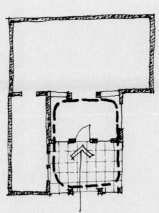

Imagine the entry as a single room bisected by the front door.

In the rainy Pacific Northwest, where a well-sheltered place to arrive is essential, this outdoor entry room provides plenty of space to get out of the weather, find a comfortable seat, and put down packages. With the gate closed, the entry can contain pets and small children.

*Place rooms along a privacy gradient,
with the most public spaces near the entry,
the most private spaces more remote.*

PASSAGE: MOVING THROUGH HOME

Animals create a den to provide a secure place where they can raise their young and sleep in peace. When they leave this space to move about in the world, they adopt a posture of great alertness, investigating their surroundings carefully before moving farther. For animals, this level of attention is essential for survival. As humans, we have not lost the natural sense that cautions us to move through unfamiliar spaces with great awareness or the need to create safe tucked-away spaces as retreats.

We organize our homes along an "intimacy gradient" that places the most private, most secure places at the end of the passages through the house, beyond gateways, through many boundaries. The main entry admits a visitor only to the most public end of the gradient. Within the home, we use the forms of doorways and passages to create clear messages about the degree of privacy beyond. This gradient allows us to experience the house and its surroundings as a series of layers, with its deepest secrets and greatest safety at the farthest reach.

Within passages, people pay more attention to what is happening along the edges than at the centers. We are concerned with the texture of the floors and with being able to see our objective. Circulation spaces are typically not furnished, so the details of the space itself take on added importance. Knowing this, we can focus attention on the details of surfaces and lighting to create a sense of safe passage. Through careful design, passages can have the potential to be enjoyed for their own merit, offering brief stops at a window seat, bringing attention to a surprising view or a piece of art, providing storage and browsing space for a library or a gallery of images.

Bookshelves used as guardrails along the side of this stair hall in the Limerick house make effective use of space that would otherwise be devoted simply to passing through. By adding color and interest to the edges, they enliven the entire stair.

Lined with books and windows, this passage connects the main entry with two home offices and provides access to the garden. The space acts as a second entry, a strategy that supports the intimacy gradient in two ways: First, visitors to the offices do not need to enter the main house, and second, the physical separation of the offices places them in the least public zone of the house. This house (by the authors) is discussed in more detail in Pattern Seven.

RIGHTS OF PASSAGE

- Make the circulation efficient by routing traffic through a central point, using the shortest passages possible to reach rooms.

- Circulate along the edges of the common spaces of the house, bringing passersby into view of the rooms but not close enough to interrupt activities within.

- Create something to walk toward or to walk along— a reason to be there besides passing through.

- Take advantage of turns and changes of level to emphasize arrival in a new setting.

- Pay attention to light; use it to draw people forward, to highlight an intersection, to dramatize a stopping place, to create safe level changes.

- Include elements of the spaces the passage connects, but also make sure that the passage is defined architecturally as an independent area.

Travel along the edge of this family dining area connects everyone with the heart of the house yet leaves activities there uninterrupted. A beam, high overhead, subtly defines the edge of the circulation zone, and interior windows mark both end points.

THE STAIRWAY PASSAGE

Stairs can provoke intense responses. The grand staircase is a staple of movie sets and expensive tract homes, encouraging visions of a glamorous entrance or a significant retreat. Children have memories of hiding halfway down the stairs to watch adult activities below, and teenagers recall sneaking upstairs after hours. What is it about stairs that provokes these intense responses? And how can we design them so that they encourage the experiences that lead to fond memories and still meet our budget and space demands?

The staircase itself can be a useful, dramatic space, with a profound impact on the floor plan. Staircases can be the focal point of all the circulation in the house; located near the entry, they can add height and drama to the space where people arrive. On upper floors, stairs can arrive at a generous hall that serves several rooms rather than at a narrow hallway. There are a variety of ways to create memorable staircases.

- Design a stairway to enhance the experience of a change in level, marking progress by providing interior windows to domestic views or windows that look out of doors and capture the sense of change in elevation.

- When possible, create stairs that twist or turn. The change of viewpoint adds interest to the trip, and the shorter runs reduce the chance of injury in case of a fall.

- Look for natural stopping points. A window seat at a landing or an overlook to rooms below creates an opportunity to slow down or a place to stop and rest.

- Walls located opposite the top or bottom of the stairway are natural locations for objects of special interest. Consider lighting to highlight an artwork, a niche for sculpture, or a special window to capture a view.

- Provide natural light; it highlights the edges of steps to improve safety, and the changing patterns of light and dark give definition to the forms of the staircase. Stairwells create natural shafts to bring light from above down to a lower floor; placing skylights or clerestory windows high above will fill the staircase below with light.

- Consider using stairs as seats. Where lower steps adjoin a gathering area, make the lower steps broad enough to accommodate several people; at landings, allow space for a window seat or a reading bench.

- Use a staircase to help form an edge of a space or give shape to the space around it. The activity of the stairway will enliven the rooms it adjoins, and its volume will increase the sense of space.

This is a staircase that encourages use and enjoyment of every inch. The first two steps, at the edge of a passage looking into the kitchen, work as stair seats. On the first landing of the winding stair, a child-size nook uses the space below the stairs to create a comfortable cushioned window place. At the midway landing and at the top of the stairs windows provide light and view.

- Use the space below stairs to create memorable nooks or significant storage. Let this space become an important part of the design.

- On sloping sites and in long houses, stairs can be broken into a series of short rises, allowing the building to follow the slope and serve rooms at a variety of levels.

TRANSITION: A MOMENT'S PAUSE

Within a house, transitions from one space to the next happen at many scales. The role of a transition zone is to enhance the relationship between the spaces it connects by encouraging us to pause at the threshold, to pay attention to the change. This may be accomplished by increasing the drama when the contrast is great, by tying spaces together when a link is needed, or by increasing the separation to give two spaces their own identity. The amount of area required to create this pause varies with the intensity of the transition and with the scale of the spaces being connected.

Some of the most important connections in a house are those that link outdoor rooms with the interior. Often interior and exterior spaces are designed to complement each other. Perhaps a family kitchen indoors is adjacent to a generous deck outside; together they form a setting for all the activities surrounding seasonal meal preparation and dining. But the two spaces may be very different—one climate controlled, artificially lit, contained in feeling; the other exposed to the elements, the changing light, the surrounding activities.

Moving comfortably between these spaces demands a bridge, perhaps a wide doorway into a space under a small roof or trellis that softens the change in light level and tempers the weather. But it's essential to create some space. Imagine walking outside through a sliding glass door on the lower floor of a two-story wall. The change from in to out is instantaneous, allowing no time to check out the surrounding area, no time for the eyes to adjust to outdoor light or for the body to acclimate to different temperature or weather conditions. Without a pause, the movement from space to space is immediate and harsh.

A change in floor surface from landing to stairs both improves safety by making the dropoff visible and adds architectural interest by using finishes appropriate to each space. Here, the combination of slate floors above, wood slab treads, and tongue-and-groove floors below gives each space a distinctive floor surface.

Inside the house, the transition between rooms can be elaborately marked (as in the well-trimmed opening shown above) or it can be minimal. Providing a place to collect your thoughts between rooms can be accomplished with the simplest of strategies—such as a thickened wall, thick enough that for just a moment you are really out of the room you are leaving and in a clearly separate space. In larger homes, such as the Oregon house featured next, transition spaces can become part of the rhythm of moving through the building, with enclosed spaces separating passages along the edges of rooms.

The columns that separate the kitchen and dining room in this large home by Huestis Tucker lend an air of formality, helping create a strong boundary for each room while emphasizing the point of transition and making the passage from one room to the next into a moment of ceremony.

A House for All Seasons

The balcony overhanging this walkway does double duty, offering the studio above a view to the lawn and protecting those on the path below from sun and storm. The rhythm of columns and roof beams marks progress toward the entry as well as establishing a sense of containment.

CLIMATE PLAYS AN IMPORTANT ROLE in determining how we move around a house. Where temperatures are mild and the weather temperate, outdoor rooms play a more important role, and the paths that connect rooms can be outdoors as well as in. Whereas the Ohio house presented on p. 163 has to contend with cold winters and occasional snow, this house designed by architect Jim Givens responds to the mild winters and pleasant summers of Oregon with a generous use of outdoor spaces. Cars arrive along a driveway shared with a neighbor at the lower edge of the site and park in a small car court beside the detached garage/studio building. The view toward the main house is partially screened by trees, but the path to the front door lies just around the corner, protected by the overhanging balcony of the studio above the garage. The path leads past a sloping lawn with its edges defined by the house, retaining walls, and landscape.

MARKING THE ENTRY

The front door ahead is recessed under a dormer gable and balcony—a combination that offers both protection and a symbolic marker for the entry. Before arriving at the door, the path runs between two gardens—each an outdoor room—helping define the edges and CRE-ATING ROOMS, OUTSIDE AND IN. Inside the house, this pattern is repeated where the route crosses the "hearth room," effectively forming an edge to the cooking area and to the dining space.

Inside the front door, an entry room connects through the house to the "back" door. This room is designed as a very separate space with no views into the living areas. It is not until you are invited to proceed along the passage into the hearth room that you really enter the private world of the owners. The entry room meets all the practical needs of those who arrive; it's generous enough to allow room for a table and a bench and offers a row of pegs and shelving for outdoor

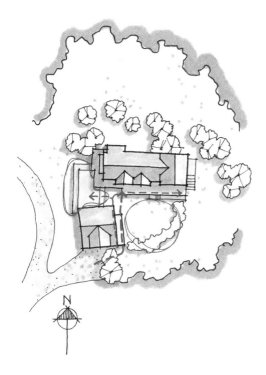

Looking up the passage along the dining room back toward the entry, a series of framed doorways and changes in level create a sense of procession. The fireplace inglenook to one side is a perfect example of Private Edges, Common Core, a cozy and defined alcove at the edge of a lively room.

Coming and going from the house you travel the edge between two distinct outdoor rooms: a large garden open to the south and east, its edges framed by trellises, walkways, and protected sitting areas, and a smaller, more intimate paved court exposed to the north and west close to the porch off the master bedroom.

The entry porch, while simple, is easy to find, well sheltered, and inviting. The gable roof centered above the door marks the spot, the double columns at each side of the recess frame the opening and tie back to the double columns at the covered walk.

garments. A laundry/mudroom with a shower sits to one side, ready to handle wet or muddy children and pets.

A SENSE OF PROCESSION

To capture views and light to the south effectively, the house is composed of rooms stretched out from east to west, stepping down the site, with circulation paths kept to the north (on the narrower upper floor) or through the middle. The result is great light in all the rooms, and a well-formed privacy gradient that creates a real sense of removal for the bedrooms and the retreat. From the entry room, a short hall steps down into the hearth room—the heart of the house—bisecting the space, with kitchen on one side and dining on the other. A few more steps lead down to the retreat.

Two strategies combine to reduce the amount of square footage devoted to circulation and to enliven the trip. First, travel along the edge of rooms ensures a changing scene and scale and allows adjoining rooms to share the space. Second, a linear route creates a strong sense of procession. On the lower floor, the trip is made up of a series

THE PATH THROUGH THE HOUSE

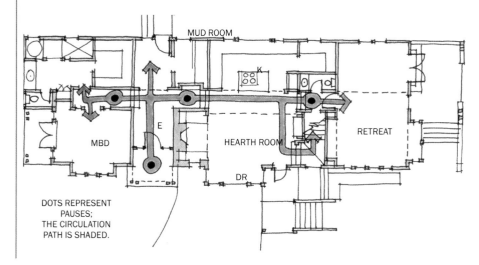

MUD ROOM

K

E

MBD

HEARTH ROOM

RETREAT

DR

DOTS REPRESENT PAUSES; THE CIRCULATION PATH IS SHADED.

of pauses (compressed halls with closed walls) and flows (open passages along the edge of active spaces). Level changes of just three steps mark the entry to each space and create a natural change in pace.

For this house, a cluster of patterns work together to create a harmonious but tremendously diverse series of spaces.

Creating Rooms, Outside and In; Parts in Proportion.

The site is broken down into outdoor rooms of several sizes—an instance of two patterns interacting to produce spaces of many scales and different characters.

Private Edges, Common Core.

The outdoor rooms are planned with this as a guiding pattern. The large sloping lawn is a generous common center with a circulation path and more private spaces along its edges; tucked around the corners and on balconies are even more private spaces—still at the edge but remote.

BRINGING IT HOME

A Graceful Flow through Rooms

Perhaps the best compliment that can be paid a circulation system is that it not only works well but makes the house a better place. The homes featured here are very different, but each invites us to enter, introduces us gracefully to the spaces within, allows passage along the edge of rooms without disturbing the activity taking place, helps us pace our flow, and facilitates our travel through the house. These houses are carefully planned so that the public portions of the site and the house are enlivened by people passing nearby, yet privacy is ensured in the inner realms of the home.

Inside, there's a powerful illustration of a family-centered commons with well-developed edges. The large kitchen/dining room at the center of the plan has four alcoves at its edges that create spaces for a variety of activities: work, study, enjoying the view. The fireplace inglenook, for instance, provides a private corner with a strong "back" against which a person can sit and look out (a spot that also works as Refuge and Outlook).

A carved truss beam marks the edge of the circulation path that separates the kitchen from the dining area. The beam contributes to a strong sense of center and gives the kitchen an independent identity.

Good houses have magnetic communal areas where people are drawn together and, connected to them at a variety of scales, rooms and places where they can be alone.

PRIVATE EDGES, COMMON CORE

This common room is strengthened by the half-private edges that suround it. The fireplace forms both a private ingle-nook and a part of the common room.

MOST HOMES ARE MADE FOR GROUPS of people. To support the social life of their residents, they must contain a balance and a variety of private and common spaces. But just because a home has these spaces doesn't necessarily mean they will work. It's the way the spaces are related that makes all the difference. For example, a private homework space won't help foster good study habits if it is too remote and children never use it. A dramatic dining room, beautifully lit and furnished but isolated from the casual flow of traffic through a house, will never become a space that draws people together and provides a focus for informal social life.

In terms of privacy and community, the rooms in conventional homes are often either/or: They are either retreats or places to gather. But while family life requires such places, it also needs places that are half private, places where a few people can talk and still be socially connected with someone who is sitting nearby reading the paper. Children often want to be "alone" in the presence of the family, and this is a need that persists in various forms throughout adulthood. Homes that support these kinds of needs with a variety of private and half-private places more and less related to the common core help their inhabitants establish a personal common/private comfort level within the family. Finding the right mix of common and private spaces, and putting them together in a way that allows both to flourish, is one of the central issues of home design.

The desk nook to the left and the inviting booth to the right form private edges serving and connecting both the kitchen and the dining room.

WORKING WITH THE PATTERN

To support the complexities of family life, houses need a balance of social and private spaces. The social places themselves should be knit together to form a strong common heart with private places at its edge.

- *Organize the main social spaces of the house*—kitchen, dining, and living/family rooms—as a single, flowing common space, with one place as its clear heart.

- *Make the heart a generous, attractive space,* just off the main circulation crossroads of the house—protected from traffic, yet located so that everyone coming and going passes by it.

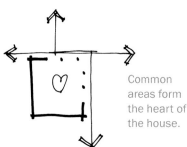

Common areas form the heart of the house.

- *Give the commons a semiprivate edge,* with places to sit and read or even just lean—places that allow people to take up a position away from the core but still be a part of it.

- In contrast to the common area at the heart, *create a sequence of private spaces,* some immediately adjacent to the heart, some relatively remote.

- *The private spaces, even at their most remote, should be conceived as edges* that give definition to the commons by the fact of separating themselves from it.

- *Create an intimacy gradient,* with a variety of corresponding ceiling heights, across the house, from the largest and highest-ceilinged commons to the most intimate and lowest-ceilinged edge.

The private areas off the commons form a sequence from least to most private. Think of the private spaces as thick edges that define and protect the commons at the heart.

The key to this pattern lies in the insight that private and common spaces work together to form a single whole: A good common space is a "center" with private edges; and a good private space is an "edge" off a common center. The photograph on p. 178—the great room of the Katul residence, a house that we'll look at in detail later in this chapter—illustrates this point perfectly. The large, high-ceilinged common area has a sitting circle as its heart; the circle is given focus by a large fireplace inglenook at its edge. The seat inside the inglenook is both a part of the sitting circle and a private place set off from it. The ingle-nook itself, a relatively thick and massive form, helps both to focus and to define the common heart and uses its very thickness to create an intense private space. The simple diagram at right clarifies this idea.

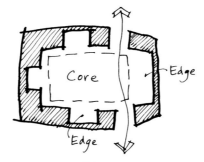

Private edges, common core—the spaces work together to form a single whole.

A bed alcove off an inglenook forms a private edge. (For another view of the inglenook, see p. 199.)

This is the view from the low-ceilinged kitchen edge back across the commons to the study. The privacy of the study is strengthened by lowering its ceiling height, by raising its floor three steps, and by marking the entry with an arch. The steps separate the study from the commons but can also serve as informal seats at the edge of the commons.

Looking from the private study at the front of the house to the eating area beyond, it's clear that the central living room is the common heart of the house. The dining table, though itself a social gathering place, is also experienced as a low and private edge off the core.

LIVING ROOM AS HEART OF THE HOUSE *The living room is a two-story center—the social and geometric hub of the house—around which private edges (work space, bedrooms, kitchen) are placed.*

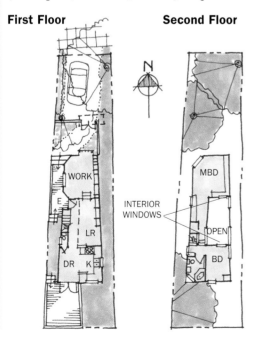

First Floor　　　　**Second Floor**

N

WORK

E

INTERIOR WINDOWS

LR

MBD

OPEN

DR　K

BD

COMMONS AT THE HEART

The Tibbetts residence, a small and elegantly designed house in Berkeley, California, by architect Glenn Lym provides a good example of this pattern. The two-bedroom house sits on an extremely narrow wedge of lot, 25 ft. at its widest (see the drawing at left). The first floor contains the major common spaces: kitchen, living, and dining areas, as well as a private work space. The two-story living room centers both the first floor and the house as a whole. Organized around the fireplace, which anchors the space, and the stairs, which animate it, the living room is the common core against which all the other spaces of the house act as edges. Each edge is less or more private, according to its position in the design. For example, the work space to the north is a private space open to the commons, whereas the kitchen/dining area to the south is a public space that opens to the commons.

Many details of the design reinforce and strengthen the overall pattern. The entrance is located at the edge of the living room, in a small recess that both gives it shape and helps separate the private work space from the center. At the top of the stairs, a bridgelike walkway

ON A SMALLER SCALE

This pattern holds true at three scales of design: first, in the house as a whole, where it can be used to organize the major common areas, indoors and out; second, on a single floor level or building wing, where it can serve to organize a cluster of rooms; and third, within a single space, where it can be used to define a room with a strong center and usable edge.

The children's bedroom shown here, created by Wyoming architects John and Nancy Carney, is a great example of Private Edges, Common Core at work in a single space. The bedroom, for two girls, is a square with a generous common space at its core and private bed alcoves, closets, and built-in desks for each child forming the edge of the room. The common space is centered on a shared storage wall and window place.

A curtained bed alcove and desk nook form the private edge. Materials, color, lighting, the break in the ceiling, the interior window connecting the desk space to the bed alcove—all work to intensify the privacy.

The common area at the center of the bedroom is organized around a shared window place, with storage below.

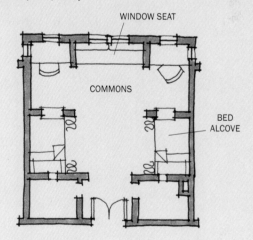

The common center is on an axis formed by the entrance and the window place at the end of the room.

The break in the kitchen counter creates a semiprivate spot, a perch that looks over the commons, part of it, yet not. This is also an interesting case, in miniature, of the pattern Refuge and Outlook.

connects the two bedrooms, which each have interior windows back into the common core. The bridge allows contact with the core and emphasizes the sense of the bedrooms as forming the most private spaces at the extreme edges of the house. The interior windows knit the rooms back to the core and deepen the sense of privacy and connection, a subtle balance quite hard to attain in a house as small as this.

The sequence of kitchen–eating–living is also organized to intensify the pattern. The kitchen/dining area together forms a low edge off the living room, but the kitchen is given slightly more separation by a solid wall above the stove and a half-open wall above a small counter. The clutter of kitchen work may be half hidden from the living room, but someone sitting at the table is visually connected to the fireplace, the kitchen, and the outdoors. This allows the table end of the room to double as both a private edge (for a child to do homework) and as an extension of the common core, where the family gathers to eat, within sight of the fireplace and the rear garden.

The kitchen is arranged to form a semiprivate edge above the living room, the social heart of the house. The stairs help enliven the edge, taking circulation past the social center but not directly through it.

KITCHEN ON THE EDGE

In the Tibbetts house, the pattern is used primarily at two scales: at the scale of the house as a whole, with the two-story vertical core, and on each floor, in the way the smaller spaces are formed as edges *off* the core. An interesting case of the pattern at work within a single space can be seen in a home in San Francisco, by the same architect. Here, the kitchen forms a semiprivate edge, a half level above the living room. And within the kitchen, a jog in the counter creates a private perch, which overlooks the living room and the view beyond. The common center is defined by its private edge, and vice versa.

Unless a house can create a rich texture of common and private spaces, it's likely to fail to support our complementary needs for privacy and community and cause subtle (and not so subtle) pressures within family life. The balance and integration of spaces called for by this pattern can be achieved in many ways. Though extremely different in design, scale, and family structure, the houses that follow offer interesting interpretations of Private Edges, Common Core.

Commons House, Private Wings

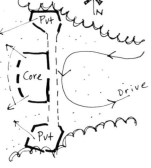

OCCASIONALLY CLIENTS come to us with projects that have so many exciting qualities that they are completely irresistible. We are swept away by the possibilities, the realities, the sheer potential. This northern California residence was such a project. The site, on a coastal range with distant views of the Pacific Ocean, is entered across a meadow from a quiet rural road. Along the north and south edges, stands of trees frame the clearing toward the ocean.

Our clients wanted a main house that would accommodate a growing family, with common areas at the heart of the house where friends could gather to cook, eat, and enjoy the views but where the owners would be equally comfortable when home alone. They also requested a comfortable guest suite, and each needed a substantial home office with space for extensive libraries and meetings with colleagues. Because the site is exposed and the climate can vary from sunny and warm to extremely stormy, we strove to create outdoor spaces that offered protection from the wind, rain, cold, and sun as well as areas that placed them fully *in* the elements.

Stringing out the buildings along a north–south axis enables each of the major spaces to be conceived as places of refuge and outlook.

WORKING WITH THE SITE

On our first visit to the site, two patterns dominated our thinking. First, the entire site with its wooded edges, gentle slope, and western exposure could be understood as a version of REFUGE AND OUT-LOOK—a creation of protected areas that allowed full enjoyment of the expansive views. Second, the pattern we're focusing on here—Private Edges, Common Core—emerged as a strategy for organizing the building along a north–south axis. The private rooms would be spread out toward the opposite ends of the axis, and the main house, with all its common spaces on the first floor, would occupy the center. Since the main house would be the largest form, the overall "massing," or shape, of the project could be imagined as a cascade of roofs stepping down from the highest point at the center to the lowest point at the edges.

When the design was completed and the house built, the overall shape and layout given to the design by thinking through this one pattern continued to hold. As you arrive

On the approach from the east (facing page), the main house with first-floor commons is in the center; the flanking wings are private spaces—office, studies, and guest bedroom.

The pattern is repeated in the vertical organization of the central building: The second and third floors are private edges with respect to the large common ground-floor spaces. The upper floors step in and contain increasingly private spaces. The third floor, with its tiniest balcony, is the private-most edge of the house.

Make the heart a generous, attractive space, just off the main circulation crossroads of the house.

The northern California residence illustrates a number of patterns of home, including the following:

Inhabiting the Site. The house spreads across the site, bringing residents into contact with the wooded edges and the middle of the meadow—the best place of outlook. But because the private wings break free of the main building instead of clogging up the site with structure, they form a necklace of indoor and outdoor rooms (Creating Rooms, Outside and In).

Sheltering Roof. The cascading roof form of the main house is one of the most memorable images of the building. And everywhere in the home, in both private and common places, the form of the roof is present. Exposed framing, sheltering eaves, and covered breezeways all establish the sense of sheltered home.

Refuge and Outlook. The string of spaces and the way they are organized, with backs and fronts, spring from our intuitive sense that this is one of the critical patterns for this site.

Places in Between. And last, the variety of balconies and porches, the breezeway, and the glazed hall are all strong examples of places in between.

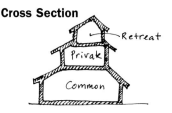

Cross Section

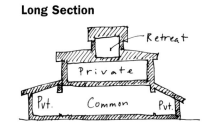

Long Section

from the east, the main house with its wings stretches across the entire clearing. The main building is a two-story structure with dormers and covered porches. A third-story roof rises near the middle of the building. Breezeways fan out from the main building. The one to the north is open and connects the front door of the main house with the guest quarters and frames the view beyond. The space to the south is a glazed hall connecting the main house and the two private studies (shown in the photo on p. 168).

FROM BOTTOM TO TOP

Not only does the pattern work as a way of organizing the house on the site, but it also holds true from bottom to top of the main house. The photo on p. 187 illustrates the "vertical" meaning of the pattern. The first floor houses all the major common spaces, which open onto a large wraparound porch on the northwest corner. (Compare the Spencer residence porch in SHELTERING ROOF [p. 81], whose form is "ruled" by the formal demands of the roof pattern, to the one shown here, where, in the grip of this pattern, it becomes a more informal element.) The long porch supports the social life of the commons and dramatically increases the usable public space.

The second floor aligns more or less with the interior of the floor below at this corner, but it seems to be stepping back, getting smaller. And *its* balcony is a smaller, more compressed version of the porch. Balconies support the private life of the house and, relative to the main floor and its large open spaces, are experienced as edges—edges that are, psychologically, away from the core. The third floor continues the pattern, stepping in to become, with its tiniest balcony, the private-most edge of the house.

The family room is open to the dining room and to the kitchen beyond. Circulation flows directly through these spaces, with many places to pause and sit along the way. To the right, are the views to the west; to the left, tucked into the back side of the commons, are places of refuge. The private/commons, pattern is, in this case, essentially fused with two other patterns: The Flow through Rooms and Refuge and Outlook.

The window bay, with its lowered ceiling, forms a private edge off an already private room—the work-space retreat at the southern edge of the site.

A SINGLE FLOWING COMMONS

The family room immediately inside the large porch is, from the point of view of social life, the heart of the house—the circle of seats drawn toward the fire. As you look to the south, through the dining room and into the kitchen, it's clear that these spaces, while certainly a part of the commons, have a kind of double identity: They are also edges off the family room core. Similarly, the wraparound porch, decidedly an extension of the common space, is also a private edge off this core. In this way, the pattern repeats itself throughout the building: Common cores have private edges, which are themselves a part of the larger space and may themselves have edges.

Looking back across the family room toward the north, you can see that that its edges are developed in the same fashion: porch, sunroom, alcove, entry bench, and raised stairway landing all support the kinds of private moments that require a niche around the common core.

Even the private offices to the south of the main building have been conceived with this pattern in mind. They possess both a social heart and a private edge, the windows becoming window bays (compare PLACES IN BETWEEN) that form more private edges to these already private retreats/studies.

Most hidden of all the first-floor private edges, a window seat is tucked in behind the stairs and the front door. The seat can double as a place to nap, a guest bed, or a place to read that's private yet still in earshot of the commons.

The private edges of the commons include the sunroom on the left, the tiny one-seat reading alcove one step up from the main floor, and the stair landing, with its rail offering a place to pause and lean.

FANNING OUT FROM THE COMMONS

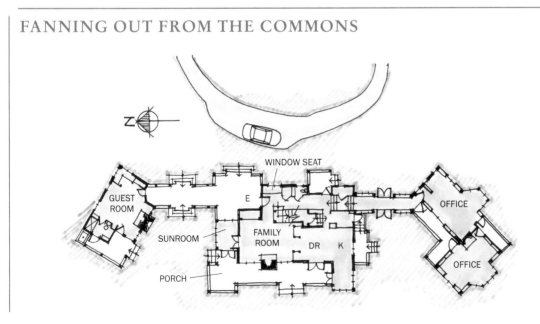

The Pattern in Miniature

The northern California residence is a large house on a large site; but this pattern can also be used to organize a small home on a small suburban lot. Shown here is a house by Oregon architects Rob Thallon and Jim Givens that includes a particularly rich blend of private and common space—from the scale of the site as a whole down to the organization of individual rooms.

The plan reveals that the dining room is the social heart of the house. The neighboring spaces—the living room and kitchen—are extensions of the common core but also private edges. The private-most edges are the studio and shop on the ground floor and the private bedrooms above.

The dining room bumps out toward a terrace in the middle of the garden—the exterior equivalent of the interior common core. The studio beyond is a private space whose edge helps define the outdoor commons.

First Floor

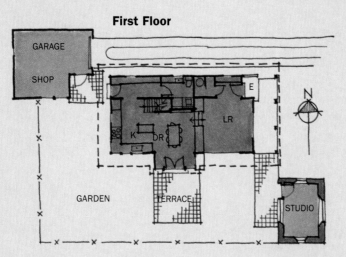

The garage/shop and the studio are the flanking wings; the dining room is the social heart, bounded by the semiprivate kitchen and living room.

Second Floor

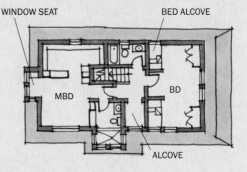

The children's room contains bed alcoves and closets that form the private edge.

The private bedrooms themselves have a common core: the small alcove at the top of the stairs, which is a place where, for example, a shared computer station might be placed. The two bedrooms offer versions of the pattern in miniature. The private window seat forms the edge to the couple's bedroom; the children's bedroom, like the bedroom shown on p. 183, contains private bed alcoves and work spaces organized around a common core. ■

The half wall and the steps down from the central dining room define the living room (in the foreground) as the semiprivate edge off the common core.

A House Full of Edges

The gable is the architectural representation of the common core of the house, while the dormers, balconies, and bays are evidence of private places on the edge.

IN THE NORTHERN CALIFORNIA HOUSE JUST DESCRIBED, we focused on the building's exterior form and showed how the private/common pattern helped establish the basic organization of the house on its site. This Oregon house by architect Jim Givens offers a chance to see the pattern at work in a variety of ways in a home's interiors.

APPROACHING THE HOUSE

The exterior of the house reveals the presence of the pattern in subtle ways. Looking up the slope toward the house, the form is basically a single long gable. The secondary building, also basically one large gable, is a garage with work studio above. In both buildings, but primarily in the main house, the simple gable form is punctured with a series of dormers, balconies, and bays. These forms give a sculpted edge to the simple gable and suggest a variety of intimate private and semiprivate spaces within. In terms of this pattern, the long gable is the core—the archetypal house itself as commons (think SHELTERING ROOF)—and the dormers, balconies, and bays are the private edges.

The path toward the front door gives a taste of what to expect on the inside. The edge of the garage is designed to create a covered walk that directs us toward the front porch, itself an elaborated edge off the main building. Rising above the porch the high gable roof is glimpsed, the common core off which everything else grows.

The main house is a simple gable form with richly elaborated edges. The garage steps down the hill to the east and has a similar form.

The exterior materials reinforce the idea of the central gable as the common core. The second-floor shingles define the gabled wall and rest on the horizontal boards of the first-floor walls.

This eating alcove is a semiprivate spot between kitchen and dining area where someone can sit with the paper (or kids can do homework) and still be part of the social life of the home.

Communal life can flow from dining room to kitchen yet still be sustained by the possibility of semiprivate life at the edge. An interior window connects the dining room and the informal booth that forms its edge.

A STRING OF COMMON SPACES

Three major common spaces—kitchen, dining, and living—interlock to form the south-facing main floor. Support spaces—hall, stairs, half-bath—are aligned and dug in to the north. Each of the three major spaces provides a variant of the pattern. The kitchen and dining room are each a kind of common core, and they share a private edge, which contains two alcoves. One is an informal place to eat, the other a desk and telephone work center that forms a circulation link between kitchen and dining (see the photo on p. 180). The subtle way the two spaces are linked draws people together for cooking, eating, and other activities and allows privacy to co-exist along with the communal action. The twin alcoves are perfect examples of PLACES IN

BETWEEN, but here we choose to emphasize how they work to establish the balance of private and common.

The living room, an elegant space that reflects a balance of formal and informal qualities, serves by itself as a case study of this pattern. To begin with, the living room is surprisingly isolated, located at the end of the hall and requiring a walk back through the hall to get to the dining room. Given the informal look of the house, the living room is more formal than you might expect. The room itself is organized along a strong north–south axis, the dark north end centered on a raised fireplace, the light south end centered on a large bay window. The strong axis adds to the sense of centrality and formality, but this quality of the space is beautifully balanced with a variety of informal gestures: The entry itself is off center and leads directly into the raised fireplace area—as though you had walked unexpectedly into an inglenook.

THREE COMMON SPACES
Each floor is an interlocking sequence of common and private spaces.

First Floor

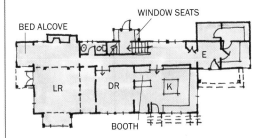

Second Floor

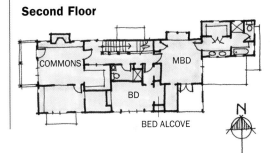

A fireplace raised two steps above the main room anchors and centers the living room. The entrance is to the right of the fireplace, so the raised level serves not only as an inglenook but also as a place to pause as you enter or leave the room.

The whole living room is a dexterous weave of center and edge. The bay window, opposite the fireplace, is both a part of the main space and a semiprivate edge.

The wall between the living room and the dining room is thickened to allow space for bookshelves and cabinets. Within this wall, the deep interior window forms yet another layer of edges—the edge of the edge is itself an edge! The leaded window alone serves as an appropriate diagram for this pattern.

Directly across from the entry, an alcove (actually a bed alcove) provides a luxuriously informal place to read, nap, or put up a guest (see the photo on p. 181). On the other side of the room, along the shared dining room wall, there is another alcovelike edge. This is for books and cabinets and contains interior (and one exterior) windows, delicately linking the hall and dining room. These windows are detailed to take advantage of the wall thickness created by the storage wall, to create an edge off the edge, so to speak.

THE PATTERN CONTINUES UPSTAIRS

The second floor of this intriguing house continues to repeat the pattern in room after room, though here, of course, the spaces are essentially private. But a couple's realm still needs private edges to support the semiprivate experience of each member of the couple. To this end, the relatively small master bedroom has a covered balcony on one side and a window seat on the opposite side of the room.

In a conventional two-story house, it's unusual to have an upstairs room that, before it is anything else, is just a wonderful room. But that is what the architect has created at the end of the hall opposite the master bedroom. Here's a room that could be many different things—office, bedroom, children's room, couple's study, studio, family room. It is directly above the living room on the ground floor and is the echo of that room, with a fireplace sharing the same chimney,

THE UPSTAIRS COMMONS
The multipurpose second-floor room is as much edge as core.

Second Floor

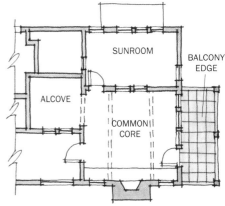

The bed is at the core of the common space in a couple's realm, but private, claimable spaces are also needed along the edge. Here, one edge is developed as a sheltered balcony, which serves as an exercise room; the other edge is a window seat.

A midlevel stairway landing is an opportunity to create a private edge, with a pair of facing window seats.

and a medley of edges to rival the living room. In effect, it is an upstairs commons, and it continues to illustrate the way in which the architect deploys this pattern not just in the kitchen and master bedroom but in virtually every space in the house.

The middle room on the upper level carves a private edge out of the adjacent roof. The resulting bedroom is small but manages in its few square feet to create a memorable space, compressing this pattern together with SHELTERING ROOF and CAPTURING LIGHT.

On the staircase along the north edge of the house, another unexpected private edge has been developed at the midlevel landing. The house is dug in on this side, and the landing provides a back door onto the sloping grade. But it also provides a pair of private windows seats—one more private edge, this one, in effect, an edge off the entire house.

In this residence, architect Givens offers a striking case of common spaces defined by private edges. The house could support the needs for both privacy and community (and the times when you want a bit of each) for a large family. Without the balance of private and common realms that we find in nearly every space, the house would be merely an assembly of rooms; it would lose the "both/and" quality that rooms and whole houses need to support the complex rhythms of privacy and community that make up family life.

A private edge carved out from under a roof is just enough space for a small bedroom, one that combines Capturing Light (the dormer) with Sheltering Roof (the bed nook tucked into the roof).

The stair landing also functions as a back-door entry room, providing access to the sloping grade behind the house.

One Great Room

THE TERM "GREAT ROOM" derives from medieval times when castles had one great space where everything happened. In houses, the great hall became the great room. Designers who have attempted to solve such problems of residential common space as the "dead" living room and the family/living room split have returned to the idea of the great room. The basic great room pattern is as follows: one room, relatively central, a crossroads of the house, with a ceiling higher than surrounding spaces, shaped perhaps by roof framing—an exciting space used for the most important family activities.

In the residence that we just looked at, there is no single great room. Quite the opposite. The architect created a sequence of rooms designed to sustain common and private family life distributed throughout the home, on the upper level as well as the main level. But in the Katul residence, the same architect, Jim Givens, has turned to the great room pattern and created an intriguing version of Private Edges, Common Core, one that contrasts nicely with the previous house and shows the range of ways the pattern can be interpreted.

The high bay window on the entry side hints at the existence of the great room within.

A MAGNETIC CENTER

In the Katul home, the great room fuses kitchen, dining, and living room into a single vaulted space of roughly 28 ft. by 23 ft. The kitchen is a pavilion within the space. Living room seating is gathered around a fireplace that is itself an inglenook, a private edge off the great room (see the photo on p. 178). The

In this view of the great room looking toward the rear of the site, the kitchen with its own open-framed ceiling is like a pavilion within the room. It is possible to be "inside" the kitchen without leaving the great room.

GREAT ROOM AT THE CENTER *The great room is a gabled space with all the adjoining support spaces organized around it like sheds around a barn.*

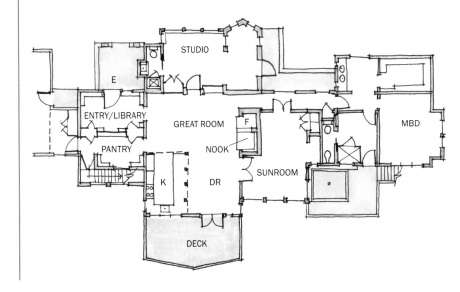

The kitchen is enclosed enough to be experienced as a distinct place—food and dishes can be kept out of view—yet it is still connected to the social life of the room.

great room is centered under a gabled ridge, the highest ridge of the house, and captures light from the rear of the site with three tiers of windows stepping in as they rise toward the ridge. At the opposite end, a single window near the ridge forms a kind of prow to the room, which from the exterior clues in anyone arriving to the existence of the interior space.

If the great room is the magnetic social space of the house, it is also a foil for the private-most edge of the house, the couple's bedroom at the far west end of the hall. As you pass through the great room en route to this bedroom, the masonry walls of the studio and fireplace compress to form a narrow threshold. The laundry and bathroom are located to "stretch out" the narrow hall and so intensify the transition into the private space. Finally, entering the bedroom, with its own window seat at the farthest edge, the bedroom is experienced as retreat, a private realm set apart from and its privacy heightened by the presence of the great room.

BRINGING IT HOME

The Balancing Act

Like ecological niches in a biocommunity, homes should provide a wide variety of settings for group and private life. And these settings should be interrelated, so that we are able to find a measure of privacy at the edge of a group space, yet still maintain a connection to the common core when we're in the private places. The two needs are not exclusive; each arises within the frame of the other, and a good house helps us find comfortable places in this critical dimension, places that give a sense of balance to our lives.

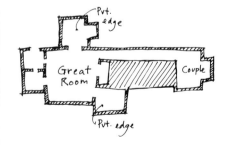

The social magnetism of the great room contrasts with the retreat and privacy created by the couple's bedroom.

The spaces that form the private edges are overlaid with use and meaning. What appears to be a library study off the great room is also the main entry to the house, a compressed gateway into the great room. The transom windows above borrow light from the main space.

REFUGE AND OUTLOOK

From time immemorial, people have needed high, secure, enclosed places from which to safely look out at the world below and beyond.

ONE OF THE FUNDAMENTAL PLEASURES that shelter offers is the sense of a solid, stable, and protected place from which you can look out over a "great beyond." This can be vividly experienced on a hike in the hills, when you finally arrive at a stone lodge that provides shelter and a view out over the landscape below. Good homes invite their inhabitants to enact this drama daily in a variety of spaces. Some examples from our everyday experience in good homes include sitting inside the house near the fire with the rain beating down on the roof and looking out the window to see the water coming down; hiding upstairs on the balcony, peering through the railing, and listening to the adults' party below; and relaxing on a covered front porch, watching life go by on the street below.

In all cases, the core of the experience is being able to comfortably observe the outer world from a position of relative security. Usually, the refuge is at a higher position and is enclosed and dark; the outlook is normally below, unenclosed, and lighter. At its simplest, we are inside, looking out.

Grant Hildebrand, who teaches architecture at the University of Washington in Seattle, has studied this pattern for many years. He believes that we find pleasure in the environment when it satisfies our pre-

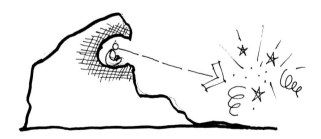

THE WRIGHT REFUGE AND OUTLOOK

Many of Frank Lloyd Wright's early Chicago houses include good examples of Refuge and Outlook. Wright placed the main level of his houses on the second story, well above street level, and set the rooms back from a low-walled patio or terrace overlooking the sidewalk. This arrangement allows the occupants of the house to venture out onto the patio from inside and to overlook the street life without being seen by passersby.

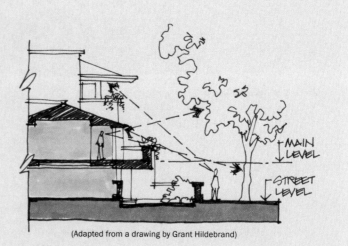

(Adapted from a drawing by Grant Hildebrand)

Children (and cats) love to get into small enclosed spaces in which they can hide and look out. For a Toronto child-care center, the authors used the notion of refuge and outlook to design these house-like play structures, which provide opportunities for climbing up into an enclosed refuge that can either be defended against "attackers" or be used as invitations for "visitors."

historic physical needs. For example, as a relatively weak and vulnerable species, we needed to gain shelter and protection in a position where we could oversee and anticipate external dangers and opportunities. Hildebrand points out that the raised terraces in Frank Lloyd Wright's prairie houses enable the residents to look out over street life without allowing people on the street to look into the hearts of these houses.

This instinct to locate oneself in a safe, easily controllable position that permits observation of the wider world beyond is very deep. Understanding this can help us do a better job of designing buildings.

WORKING WITH THE PATTERN

Beyond simply providing physical shelter and safety for our bodies and possessions, a house must meet our psychological needs for shelter and safety: In a truly comfortable house, the inhabitants will *feel* sheltered and safe. Combined with this sense of refuge must be the opportunity for prospect, for a view out, overlooking the wider world beyond. Based on our deep and ancient experience as hunters, we need the experience of being able to look out and down on the outside world from a protected position of advantage and safety.

- *Include spaces that are thick and massive feeling,* enclosed, and with a solid back.

- *Try to make the users less visible from the outer world* by keeping the light level lower, by providing screening shades and plants, or by giving the users a deep space into which they can withdraw.

- *In general, position areas of refuge and outlook* somewhat above the level of the view beyond, so that they provide an overlook.

- *The spaces should temper the climate,* offering either summer coolness (like a covered porch) or winter warmth (like a sunlit bay window) to encourage longer and more frequent use.

The house should incorporate a range of spaces that simultaneously permit holding back for protection and reaching out for observation; that offer deep, secure retreats combined with the possibility of observing more exposed, brightly lit prospects.

FROM LARGE SCALE TO SMALL SCALE

Our firm applied this pattern in a house in Inverness, California, at both a large and a small scale. The house has deep, enclosed outdoor decks that offer views out over the gently descending gardens below. The upper deck is carved out of the house and roof, firmly sheltering the viewer and creating a strong sense of refuge (see the photo at right).

On a smaller scale, in the interior of the same house, it is possible to overlook the action in the living room from the privacy and shelter of the bedroom a half story above through an interior window linking the two spaces. The opening is fitted with pocket shutters when more privacy is desired. As a bonus, this device helps increase the visual size of the bedroom, at the same time adding interest to the living room (see the photo at left on p. 210).

This house in northern California was conceived as a secure enclosure from which the owners could have protected views out to the landscape below.

The interior of this house offers many opportunities for refuge and overlook. You can overlook the living room from the refuge of the hallway, the bottom of the stairway, the upstairs balcony, or even from a secret opening above the bookshelf.

An interior window provides prospect from the refuge of the master bedroom, which overlooks the living room.

In our design for the Thomas residence in Oakland, California, the opening between the main stairway and the living room is designed to permit a variety of contacts between the two spaces (see the photo above). You can sit on the lower steps and be seen or a little higher up and be hidden. At the top landing, a projected balcony creates an additional set of possibilities. Children can sneak up there and secretly observe and listen in on the adult conversation or, for a very special occasion, the owners can make an announcement or offer a toast to the crowd assembled below.

The range of this pattern can extend from the siting and orientation of the house all the way down to small enclosed alcoves that look out into a larger room. In the following example, the whole house can be thought of as a refuge with an overlook of the ocean beyond.

LOOKING OUT OVER THE OCEAN

Architect Bernie Baker was working with a magnificent lot overlooking Puget Sound, Washington, but in a climate that can turn very windy and wet. At the largest scale, his design for the house creates Refuge and Outlook by the way the building sits on the downsloping site. The house has a level floor, a bit dug in on the entry side and gradually becoming an elevated pad at the rear, downhill view side. Looking back at the house from below, you can see that it forms a strong "back" from which to experience the open views beyond. The living room on the right, the small protected courtyard in the middle, and the couple's bedroom on the left are arranged in a U shape, like a cave, that leads out to a raised terrace at the rear. On the terrace, the small central courtyard is the refuge, and the terrace itself provides the outlook.

This same pattern is applied again at the smaller scale of the individual rooms, as in the master bedroom, where the pattern is used to underscore the sense of privacy and intimacy of this area. The bed is deep in the room, with its back against solid wall near a reassuring fireplace. The view is directly across the foot of the bed, accentuated by the thrust of the ceiling beams, open wall, and terrace beyond.

This house on Puget Sound steps back from the view a bit and sits on a solid terrace platform, which provides a raised overlook of the water beyond. But the house also offers an opportunity for withdrawal and refuge.

The heart of the interior is the massive fireplace with its low ceiling, chunky framing, and small windows, all lending a great sense of security and refuge to the house in winter.

REFUGE AND OUTLOOK FOR ALL SEASONS

Far from the ocean, set deep in the heart of the California Sierra Nevada Mountains, a family cabin provides a similarly rich mix of refuge and outlook opportunities. The architect, George Homsey, clearly has a deep understanding of how to integrate a building to its site to enable the residents to enjoy life there in all seasons. We'll look at this house again in COMPOSING WITH MATERIALS, but here we want to focus on how the architect has created two versions of refuge and overlook, one for the deep snowy winters, another for the warm summers.

The winter version of the pattern begins at the living room with the large stone fireplace on the north wall, its massive rocks, concrete mantel, chunky timbers, and tiny low windows combining to create a secure, cavelike refuge. The most protected refuges are often smaller spaces for a few people just off larger more common spaces, a feature of this pattern that is closely related to the pattern PRIVATE EDGES, COMMON CORE. This fireplace is a good example.

As you move across the room toward the south, light and view start to pour into the room from the continuous skylight and window, a bright, high-ceilinged end of the room that promises a prospect beyond. This pattern is often related to CAPTURING LIGHT, too, because views out to a larger prospect are usually associated with

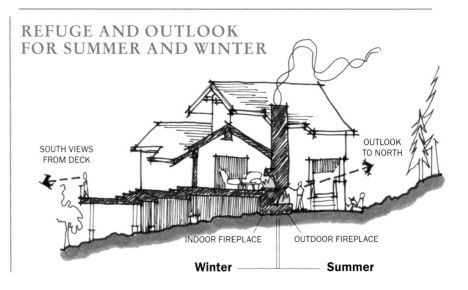

REFUGE AND OUTLOOK
FOR SUMMER AND WINTER

SOUTH VIEWS
FROM DECK

OUTLOOK
TO NORTH

INDOOR FIREPLACE   OUTDOOR FIREPLACE

Winter ———————— **Summer**

The **south side** of this same room is high ceilinged, with a magnificent skylight united with a view window. This light leads to a vista beyond and below, accessible from the southern deck just outside this window.

Stepping out and down from the house, you emerge onto the deck, which offers a gradually unfolding view that is fully appreciated when you reach the edge of the railing.

The summer version of the refuge begins with the outdoor fireplace, its outlook framed by the surrounding building.

higher light levels (see the photo on p. 213). The deck just outside steps down gradually, leading farther and farther out toward the view of a lake beyond. At the end of the deck, quite high above the ground, is the full view out over the whole landscape.

Looking at the drawing on p. 212, you can see that there is also a summer version of this pattern, beginning at the outdoor fireplace, which is built back-to-back with the living room fireplace. This is the northern, cooler side of the house, and the refuge originates, again, with the fireplace. But here, the outlook opens up and outward to the north and the hills behind the house, as the ground rises up gradually to form an amphitheater.

Porches on both sides of this amphitheater, from the dining room on the left and a private bedroom on the right, pump life into this courtyard (CREATING ROOMS, OUTSIDE AND IN). As night falls, a fire in the outdoor fireplace, together with the embrace of the surrounding building, creates a safe harbor from which the sounds and mystery of the nightfall can be enjoyed.

Three Nested Overlooks in the Pacific Northwest

REFUGE AND OUTLOOK CAN BE APPLIED at many scales within the home, from siting to the arrangement of the major divisions of the building down to the layout of smaller spaces. The house we look at here incorporates an entire hierarchy of uses of the pattern.

The homeowners resettled on Vashon Island near Seattle after many years of living in a white-painted, 1880 Victorian house with 11-ft. ceilings in Connecticut. They chose Tom Bosworth as their architect because of his ability to translate the vocabulary of traditional architecture (with which they were already comfortable) to the landscape of the Pacific Northwest. They wanted a house that incorporated traditional forms on the outside but was countrified and more relaxed on the inside—an elegant, yet informal, house.

The separate buildings are a related family of traditional forms, their backs up against a group of trees, each looking out toward the view. Each building has a covered porch that's slightly different from the others.

This porch, with its overview of the land beyond, has all the elements required for refuge—back wall with doors for further retreat, generous depth, cover, a screen of columns and railing, and raised height.

THREE HOUSES *The home is composed of three "houses"—bedrooms, commons, and studio—all set out roughly perpendicular to the slope, all oriented toward the views below.*

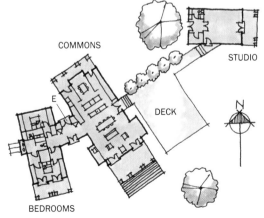

THE HOUSE RESPONDS TO THE SITE

The site is a meadow, sloping gently down to the south and west toward a view of the water. The house plan was developed as three separate structures—commons, bedrooms, and studio. These three pieces are linked together on the site by geometry, circulation, and a little bit of structure, but they retain their individuality and shape interesting spaces in between (CREATING ROOMS, OUTSIDE AND IN). The central commons is the largest of the three buildings, and the other two are organized along its cross axis. This site plan is a good example of INHABITING THE SITE because it creates opportunities to extend the inhabitants' observations and activities out into the landscape.

Looking back up at the building complex from below, it's possible to see the Refuge and Outlook pattern expressed in the site plan itself. The individual buildings are grouped together but face off into slightly different directions, corresponding to the slope of the land. Each building looks down nearly perpendicular to the slope, while huddling back toward one another against the slope and the protecting trees to the north. From this secure, higher position back against the grove, their orientations are individual and relaxed, but also watchful, looking out to the open land below.

Each of the three buildings is a simple rectangle, aligned toward the view and culminating in a deep porch. While the buildings and porches are different in function, size, and plan, they share common features, following the pattern PARTS IN PROPORTION. This variety within an overall unity ensures that the complex has a fresh and lively composition. Because the buildings are rotated in the site plan, each porch gets a subtly different view; the main house points directly at Mount Rainier. This slight turning away from each other gives each a sense of privacy and expansiveness.

PORCH PROTECTION

The porches constitute another version of the refuge pattern at a smaller scale. Defined by a rear wall, the roof, and the four columns at the outside edge, they have an enclosing, protected shape. They are given the additional important features of doors at the back to allow further retreat in cool weather and a raised elevation to increase the amount of overlook.

The commons porch works as a strong refuge as a result of several key features provided by the architect:

- a solid wall behind

- doors in the wall leading to the interior

- a generous 12-ft. depth

- a solid roof overhang

- substantial support columns

- raised height above the ground (around 18 in.)

- a railing surrounding the edge

All of these small design features combine to create the convincing overall sense of refuge, from which the owners can command the view beyond. They are probably not going to be attacked by seafaring invaders, but the porch design does embody some classic defensive design strategies. That understanding provides a real psychological basis for the feeling of security, comfort, and pleasure provided by the porches. Exploring this imaginary attack further, the solid wall behind creates a wind barrier and a physical back that gives a sense of security (because enemies must attack from the front). The doors leading to the interior of the house offer a

The porch is so substantial and sheltering that it encourages the owners to fully enjoy the wind and rain, sun, and action of the overview beyond.

retreat if things get too rough. The generous depth allows room to gather in force or to hang back from the edge if greater stealth is desired. The covered roof prevents attack from above and creates a darker space underneath for better camouflage. You can even hide behind the beefy columns. The raised floor height increases defensibility by permitting a longer view out into the vast unknown. Finally, the railing is an actual barrier to entry and forces access at the narrow, more defensible stairs at the edges. The well-designed porch is the grown-up version of the childhood fort.

The sheltered U-shaped outdoor space formed by the bedroom and commons wings and the entry is also protected enough to serve as a refuge from the larger space beyond.

SHAPING THE OUTDOORS

Beyond the porch, the pattern of refuge and outlook is at work in several other places in this house. The outdoor space created by the entry, commons, and bedroom can be thought of as an outdoor, room-size version of a refuge. This space has all the features listed for the porch except the roof and columns. The landscaping at the edges almost takes on the role of a railing, providing some "defense" at the front edge of the space. It's also noteworthy that the space flares out, providing a wider angle of view. This minor opening up of the space, only around 15 degrees more than the 90 degrees of a rectangle, is a subtle gesture that actively orients and points the space toward the view beyond.

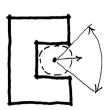

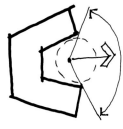

Opening one side of an enclosed outdoor space slightly creates an orientation toward that opening and more strongly invites the outdoors in.

This flaring has its complement on the front entrance side, where the surrounding wings necessarily point inward, creating a gatewaylike transition at the edge and then a directional widening as the arriving visitor approaches the door.

From inside the entry, this semiprotected outdoor space looks secure and invites us to move out farther toward the view.

The guest arriving at the entry proper first passes through the narrow gateway of the angled wings and then is "released" to move toward the front door.

REFUGE AND OUTLOOK INSIDE THE HOUSE

Moving inside the house, there are a number of examples of the pattern at work, including the arrangement of the master bedroom. From the bed backed up against an interior wall, the owners can look out at the prospect, but from an even deeper spot inside the refuge of the house. Similarly, in the commons wing, the most public activities (formal living and dining areas) are up at the porch end, whereas the more private and intimate spaces (kitchen and breakfast) are back deeper into the house. Thus, from the refuge of the open kitchen deep in the heart of the house, there's an overlook of the entire public social area of the house, the porch beyond, and the landscape beyond that.

GOING BEYOND THE PATTERN

The pattern THE FLOW THROUGH ROOMS has an interesting expression in this house. While the exterior of the entry is a small, protected porchlike space, the interior is both a passage, linking its two wings, and a pleasant space in its own right, filled with light and access to a south-facing deck beyond.

This house in the Pacific Northwest is not only a great example of Refuge and Outlook but also does a wonderful job of creating Parts in Proportion. As discussed in that chapter, nature offers a powerful basis for good proportion in the formula "create balance around an axis of development." The simplest architectural response is the establishment of a dominant center surrounded on each side by a secondary element. Examples include a large window flanked by two smaller windows and a tall central building in between two shorter ones. This simple formula always starts with three elements and then proceeds to subdivide, often down through several levels of detail.

As illustrated here, the pieces of the Vashon Island house are proportioned in thirds throughout—in plan, section, and elevation—and at many different scales: the three main wings, the three parts of each wing, the three zones in section, and so on. The effect is an apparent harmony and balance, not only in the big gestures but also continuing deep into the details of the design.

Plan

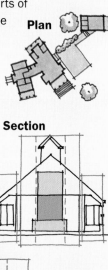

Section

Elevation

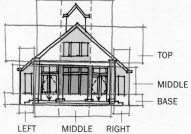

TOP

MIDDLE

BASE

LEFT   MIDDLE   RIGHT

All the functions in the central commons house are arranged in a sequence that runs from the most protected—the kitchen—through the dining and living areas, to end at the covered porch.

The house is also designed with a strong sense of the commons at the heart of the complex (PRIVATE EDGES, COMMON CORE). This is expressed at both the large scale (the commons building at the center with bedroom and studio buildings at the sides) and within the commons building itself. As you come into the commons from the entry, you begin to see the kitchen and breakfast dining alcove toward the north. A great room on the south contains the dining room proper, living room, central fireplace, and flanking alcoves (one for the piano, one for a reading chair).

The central spine of the commons building has a higher ceiling than the surrounding aisles of circulation and private alcoves. This central area contains the core of each function—sitting, dining, working in the kitchen, breakfast—and is, in effect, the commons of the commons. In addition, an even higher lightwell is located over the core, further centering it with unexpected natural light. The architect has established a nested hierarchy built around the central commons. The lower-ceilinged edges and corners contain the support spaces— pantry, mudroom, alcoves—and secondary circulation. The pattern PRIVATE EDGES, COMMON CORE can perhaps be thought of as the

The bedroom end of this passageway is marked with an intentional pause; two steps up and a forced turn to the right or left indicate the privacy of this wing.

From the entry, the path left through the commons and on to the studio passes gracefully between the kitchen to the left and the dining table to the right, without disturbing the activity in either space.

The dining alcove can be thought of as a more private edge to the common core of the kitchen.

Similarly, the piano alcove is a private edge off the common core of the main dining area.

interior version of Refuge and Outlook. The reading and piano alcoves, for example, are small, low-ceilinged, relatively protected spaces that you can back into and from where you can look out onto the larger, higher, more active central space beyond.

The lightwell is just one example of the many powerful ways in which this house CAPTURES LIGHT. At the porch ends, light enters the commons through a virtual wall of glass, composed of windows that reach almost down to the floor along with French doors, all topped with transom windows (see the photo at right on the facing page). These unusual windows were inspired by the owners' visit to Monticello, in which Jefferson brought his tall windows low enough to the floor that you can step through them. An unusual opening in the gable end of the porch roof (described by Bosworth as a "light key") brings more light into the upper portion of the porch and, in turn, more light into the commons through the high transom windows (see the photo on p. 217).

Light is also introduced into the commons from the side alcoves through windows on all sides of these bays. And finally, light is brought in from above, through a roof-mounted cupola that drops light separately onto the breakfast area and the kitchen. The light key focuses light on the living area via a raised ceiling (see the photo on p. 220). This house's ability to bring precious light from the often-overcast days into the interior rooms and the elegance of its organization are the features the owners value most.

Architect Tom Bosworth used many of the design patterns that we are highlighting in this book in his creation of this Pacific Northwest home. Here, the patterns are expressed in the language of traditional forms—right angles, symmetry, and simplicity of form. In the next house, we will see many of these same patterns, but expressed in a more informal, rustic language.

A cupola high above the heart of the commons—the kitchen—captures the precious Pacific Northwest light.

A Rugged, Rocky Retreat

The juncture between the building and the ground is very poetic, expressing the strength of the connection. The plants find refuge at the base of the building, just as the occupants do within it. Once refuge is established, we welcome the opportunity of outlook, here promised by the delicate window shades of metal rods, like eyelashes shading the view.

The house grows out of its site, gaining solidity and security by using the surrounding rock to link it to the outcroppings of the landscape. But it also steps boldly out to take in views of the Llano River winding around it below.

MARK CHANDLER TRAVELS A LOT and has a passion for the outdoors, but he also has a great need for a solid home base when he is not on the road. He asked architects Ted Flato and John Grable of Lake/Flato to create a house with a strong connection to the landscape of his site on the Llano River in central Texas. He wanted to be able to experience the surrounding nature fully, from a building that would sit comfortably in the especially stark beauty of the land. Seeking inspiration from historical buildings, the architects recalled the Glen Alpine Springs health camp dining structure designed by Bernard Maybeck in 1921. This building is both rooted in its landscape and open to the surrounding views—a wonderful example of Refuge and Outlook. This historical building became the seed from which the design grew (see "Inspiration from the Past" on p. 226).

SHELTER FROM THE STORM

The experience of outlook is amply provided by the house site, which sits 60 ft. above the river. Because the house is exposed to powerful storms from the west, which are channeled by the river valley and up the hill toward the house, enjoyment of the site requires powerful compensatory gestures to create refuge, a sense of safety from the storm, and protection from the brute force of nature. Whereas Maybeck's dining hall in the woods was a refuge from deep snow and cold, this building needs to be a refuge from blowing winter storms as well as from summer heat and blazing sun. The necessary refuge is provided by the physical mass of the house and its deep shaded overhangs.

Fieldstone from the property was used to form massive piers, which support the main commons roof and the wide, deep, dark balconies. The rock base structure of the house is a continuation of the steep rock cliffs of the site itself. This sense of solidity and connection to the ground is intensified by the fact that the house is not set on top of the highest hill, where it would be fully exposed, but partway down, allowing the hills behind to form a more solid back to the house. From within this nest of rocky piers, the deep shadows of the roof overhangs offer further protection, casting full shadows on the interiors of the building and allowing the occupants to gaze out at the wildness of the site from a sheltered, safe position.

INSPIRATION FROM THE PAST

California architect Bernard Maybeck (1862–1957) has been an inspiration for many contemporary architects, including ourselves. Many of the patterns can be seen in his work. The building shown here, the Glen Alpine Springs health camp dining room and kitchen of 1921, was designed to replace an earlier structure lost to fire. The building consists of three parts: a rectangular dining room to the left, an oval kitchen to the right, and a connecting roofed entry breezeway.

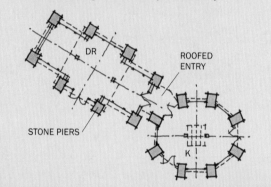

Maybeck liked to express the sheltering strength of a building, here demonstrated by the big beams, their supporting posts, and piers of concrete and rock. But this is combined with equally generous openings to the view beyond, through large steel-framed windows.

Maybeck combined massive piers built of stone from the site with factory windows and corrugated metal roofing to create a powerful gesture of rugged practicality in the wilds. The building promises security and shelter from excessive sun, wind, rain, and snow, as well as fire. But from within this rugged building, closely surrounded by the piers, beams, and metal roofing, there are magnificently open views out over the landscape through the large windows. This building is a clear expression of Refuge and Outlook.

Maybeck made a fireproof building using dry-laid stone from the site, factory windows, and corrugated metal roofing. The building is currently undergoing restoration by a group of volunteers.

A PLAN FOR PROTECTION AND PROSPECT

The plan of the house is simple, with the oval-shaped living/dining room separated from a long rectangular wing of bedrooms by a central entry/kitchen "joint" linking the two. One of the advantages of stretching the bedrooms out into a long rectangle is that each room gets an unobstructed view on two sides, with no other rooms looking into them. With no wasteful halls, residents leave the commons and walk outside under a long porch to get to their private bedroom. This porch, because of its generous depth, takes on the feeling and function of an outdoor room (CREATING ROOMS, OUTSIDE AND IN).

The porch itself provides a wonderful combination of refuge and overlook. The refuge is offered most deeply in the retreat of the private rooms themselves, which then open out to the porch and offer seating against the solidity of the wall, under the deep, dark roof overhang of exposed framing and corrugated metal. Here, a vast landscape can be taken in—from the safety of the benches against the wall or from the more adventurous and "risky" benches at the edge of the deck, well above the ground below.

The combined sense of protection and opportunity for outlook is preserved in the interiors, with the living room offering an especially rich mixture of these extremes. The fieldstone piers are as much a part of the interior experience as of the exterior. Like a mountain citadel, the walls are simple stone piers, interrupted with periodic expanses of glass. Against the back wall, the piers gather together to form an incredibly solid fireplace, the most massive and hearthlike spot in the building.

From inside the living room, there's a sense of security looking out and down to a vast and wild landscape. The surrounding massive solid structure, along with deep window screens, frames and limits the intensity of the view to manageable proportions.

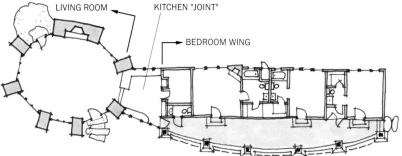

LIVING ROOM   KITCHEN "JOINT"

BEDROOM WING

The stone fireplace is the heart of the living room and is perhaps the most secure of the various spaces in the house. It combines all the features of refuge—massiveness, enclosure, darkness, and low ceiling.

The deep porch permits a wide range of exposure to the overlook, from the bedrooms that step down onto it, to the seating up against the back wall, to the loosely arranged armchairs, to the bench at the edge. The thinness of the metal roofing contrasts nicely with the solidity of the walls and rock piers, and its color gives the space some sparkle, which is a nice contrast to the earthy stone and wood.

The kitchen/entry is open to the living/dining room, but as the plan shows, it's clearly outside the strong circle of stone piers that define that space. In fact, the kitchen area is treated as somewhat of an exterior space, similar to Maybeck's Glen Alpine entry, perhaps to emphasize the refuge quality of the living room. This outdoor feeling is created by several factors: The room is outside the oval of stone piers; the use of white cabinets, metal furniture, and the window seat brightens the space; and the glimpse of the corrugated roofing material of the living room oval suggests that the kitchen is part of a later addition to the building.

VIEW FROM THE ROCK

Looking back at the exterior of the house, it's evident that the bases of the limestone piers are widened, flowing out like broadening feet to gain a better foothold into the ground. These bases then smoothly extend even farther out to form the stepping-stone path around the building and garden areas for native plants (INHABITING THE SITE).

The strong bases of the exterior piers amplify the expression of the building as a place of refuge, safety, and security. They reassure us that the building can provide shelter. And this is again expressed in the smaller detail of the plants thriving in the stone pockets formed in the space between the piers. The building gives the impression that both humans and greenery will find security in its shelter.

The exterior of the house speaks not only of refuge but equally of outlook, with window shades extending straight out from the walls, as if the building were shading its eyes to get a better view. The overall composition of exterior materials neatly combines the rugged, primitive natural rock with the delicacy of manufactured metal roofing and siding as well as trellises of timber, pipe, and recycled oil-field rods (COMPOSING WITH MATERIALS).

The kitchen doubles as the entry and, like Maybeck's Glen Alpine lodge after which this house was modeled, emphasizes the outdoors quality of this transition space. This is done by brightening the room with white cabinets, metal furniture, and a window seat and by providing the glimpse of metal roofing above the entry to the living room.

BRINGING IT HOME

A Protected Vantage

A really satisfying house should offer a sense of refuge, security, and safety in conjunction with an opportunity to reach out, explore, and overlook the greater world beyond. It has nothing to do with a particular site or location. It is as important for a city house to have an opportunity for a view of the lively street action below as it is for a house in the country to look out over the landscape beyond. Whether it's a brownstone stoop in New York City, a front porch in Denver, or a sheltered deck in Montana, each is an expression of the dual need for refuge and outlook. Every house needs to provide security, but also opportunity. Houses can, and often do, err on one side or another—either too much refuge, or too much outlook. What is needed is a balance between the two.

Every house needs places that allow you to inhabit the edge and offer enough exposure to make you aware of your surroundings and enough protection to make you comfortable.

PLACES IN BETWEEN

A generous loggia is created between the columns that support the roof and the inner wall of this Florida house. The deep overhang of this western exposure shelters the interior from direct sun late in the day, while the use of cool white paint spreads indirect light throughout the space.

OUR SCHEDULES ARE FILLED WITH ACTIVITIES, and our homes are filled with things that need to be done. For some of us, each room is a reminder of the tasks to be accomplished and the garden, a call to action. What we need are places where we can stop and take a deep breath, places in between the coming and going, the planning and the acting, the indoors and the outdoors. We seek places that are a part of daily life, where we can pause, step out of the mainstream, and enjoy the quiet eddies along the margins. As we saw in CREATING ROOMS, OUTSIDE AND IN, a good house contains well-shaped rooms that are both inside and outside. But it also needs places that are in between, half in and half out.

In-between spaces can take many forms: porches or balconies, large bay windows or tiny window seats, alcoves or sunrooms tacked on to the side of the building. Their defining quality is the sense that they exist *in addition to* the major rooms of the house; they are not essential to the function of the house but complement it.

WORKING WITH THE PATTERN

Every house needs places that fall between the inside and the outside—places where we can experience the outdoors at the same time as we enjoy the comfort and protection of the indoors. To really allow us to experience being in between, the spaces must encourage stopping, not simply passing through.

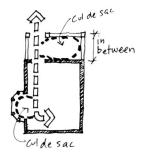

Make sure that some places in between are cul-de-sacs, with traffic passing by, not through.

Outdoor places in between need to be clearly defined as a room. Use a roof, columns, or wall elements to imply containment.

Located above the front entry, this balcony is sheltered by a projecting gable roof that both creates a strong sense of enclosure for the balcony and forms a marker for the entrance below.

▪ *Design places in between as cul-de-sacs,* quiet pools with no through traffic. Equip them with seats, make them comfortable to invite lingering, and keep traffic flow to the edge.

▪ *Make sure that interior places in between feel truly surrounded by the outdoors;* otherwise they'll be just another room. When you are within them, your connection to the outside should be as strong as to the inside. Accomplish this by actually popping the space out from the building's walls, as in a dormer or a bay window, or by making the edges of the space transparent enough that the outside appears to be barely held off, as in sunrooms or porches.

▪ *Exterior places in between must provide some of the security and comfort* associated with being indoors. Use structural elements—columns, roof, elevated floor—to imply enclosure and to create a sense of containment. Add furniture, finishes, and lighting that offer an indoor level of comfort.

▪ Although places in between vary widely in size and comfort, *they must remain as secondary spaces,* adjuncts to the primary rooms (inside or outside) they are associated with.

▪ *Design in-between places to suit the local climate* and the seasons of use. For warm-weather use, create rooms or areas that have roofs to keep the rain out, but keep the walls open or lightly screened so that the temperature and breezes can be felt. Where rain is not a concern, consider a room surrounded by walls but open to sky. For colder seasons, create indoor places that feel as if they reach outside the walls of the house and connect them directly to the outdoors through windows and skylights.

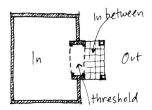

▪ *Pay attention to the boundary.* Defining the edges between the interior and the in between creates a change in awareness. Create thresholds, soffits, or frames to emphasize the change of place.

Pay attention to the moment of passing from inside to in between and mark it architecturally.

Southern porches are quintessential in-between places; they offer moments that feel apart from time and out of space, demanding nothing but promising peace. The choice of a traditional sky blue color for the ceiling emphasizes the connection to the outdoors.

THE FRONT PORCH: OUTSIDE BEING IN

The southern front porch is the archetypal place in between, perfectly suited for "just sitting," located on the fringe rather than at the center of the action, comfortable without being fussy. Neither indoors nor out, the porch is nonetheless a real room with a ceiling, walls implied by corner posts and rails, and a wooden floor. It has a view over the street or out to the garden, and it is just off the path to the entry of the house, keeping it in contact with the comings and goings of the household. The furnishings are designed to invite lingering and to encourage relaxing—rocking chairs, gliders, and porch swings are not meant for hard work. The porch adds to the life of the house and makes very few demands in return.

The classic front porch isn't limited to the South. The house shown at right by Huestis Tucker Architects is situated in the northeastern United States and is composed of traditional regional forms, but its porch affords all the comfort associated with warmer settings. Wrapping a south-facing corner, with a view out over the water, the porch combines a comfortable spot for sitting with a protected front entry.

By wrapping around the corner of the house, this front porch creates both a graceful entry and an inviting outdoor room overlooking the water. Carving the porch into the volume of the house increases the sense of protection from wind and weather in this northeastern setting.

CREATING THE PERFECT PORCH

There are several things you can do to create a porch that will become an important part of daily life. Plan from the outset to create a space that can accommodate the activities that are central to your lifestyle.

- Locate the porch so that it is visible and readily accessible in the course of ordinary comings and goings; using the porch should not require planning, it must be available on impulse. Windows looking from interior spaces onto the porch increase the sense of connection and invite use.

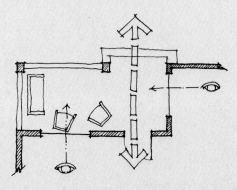

- The porch should be open to people moving in and out of the house. Treat at least part of the porch as a cul-de-sac or dead end to ensure that traffic flow moves along the edges without disturbing ongoing activities.

- The porch needs to be big enough to accommodate comfortable places to sit and to allow people to move around. It should be a minimum of 6 ft. deep and have the proportions of a comfortable room—roughly potato shaped, as described in Parts in Proportion.

- An important part of the pleasure of the porch is the experience of shared outlook. Define the corners with columns or partial walls to establish the edges of the space but maintain large enough openings so that the connection outside predominates.

- Plan the degree of separation from the exterior to preserve a sense of privacy for those using the porch. Railings between posts can vary from solid to nonexistent, from seat height to waist height, providing screening suitable to the location. Porches with a raised floor have a greater sense of separation.

- Because it is an outside space, a porch can benefit from being enclosed by two walls of a building. The walls control wind exposure and offer temperature-controlled surfaces that can contribute to creating a comfortable microclimate.

The details carefully address the more northern climate: The porch is carved into the building, using the walls of the house as windbreaks that create protected pockets, and the orientation ensures that some portion of the porch receives sun throughout the day.

The porch edges are designed to offer a strong sense of enclosure as well as to control the wind. The railing combines a shingled lower half with closely placed pickets and a substantial rail above; because the porch is located several steps above grade, the effect is to allow people sitting on the porch a generous view out and down toward the water, while simultaneously providing a visual screen from passersby— REFUGE AND OUTLOOK. Clusters of large columns on raised pediments mark the corners and the entry, emphasizing that though this space is out of doors it is also clearly inside the form of the house and protected by it.

BALCONIES AND DECKS

The most comfortable balconies are miniaturized versions of porches; they have the same sense of being protected by the house yet connected to the outdoors. Because balconies are projections from the wall of the house, it can be more difficult to achieve a sense of enclosure. Tucked up under a SHELTERING ROOF or recessed into a wall so that doors and part of the space are protected, a balcony can work both to extend the indoor space and to provide an overlook to views below. Too often, though, balconies are purely appendages on the outside of the wall, without a sense of being protected by the house. And with no strong connection to the interior, they tend to be too exposed to encourage real use.

Decks can feel similarly exposed. Without a strong definition of space provided by corners and a roof, they tend to feel more a part of the yard than of the house. Decks can be perfect outdoor rooms, but they rarely have the degree of connection to the house required to become effective places in between.

A variety of places in between allow for a range of activities in the lively gable end wall of this Colorado home. The upper level offers both a bay window and a tucked-in balcony with privacy, protection from the weather, and a sense of enclosure. The lower porch provides a hidden hot tub retreat with an easy connection to the yard beyond.

WINDOW PLACES: INSIDE BEING OUT

Indoors, windows can be used to create enticing places in between. The universal appeal of window seats and bay windows has made them almost a cliché in developer homes. A number of factors combine to make these spots attractive; most important perhaps is the way they combine the use of structure and light. A conventional window is treated as a hole in the wall, often located based purely on the exterior appearance of the house. The function is to provide light or a view for the room, and it is left to the homeowner to find a way to take advantage of the window with furniture placement. Window seats and bay windows are meant to be occupied and to be filled with light. They are planned from the beginning with the intent of providing a place to sit that is strongly connected through the window to the outdoors. Their form is distinct from the rest of the room—it is possible to be *in* them rather than to simply look out through them. And they invite us to slow down and really enjoy our surroundings—to pause in a place in between.

THE SEASONAL ROOM: AN EXPANDED BAY

There are many variations on the bay window. At one extreme, the bay can grow to become a whole room surrounded by windows, filled with light and looking into a natural setting. While typical bay windows are small enough to share the heat of the room they adjoin, larger versions, expanded bays surrounded by windows on three or more sides, can be hard to control thermally and may become seasonal rooms. In large older homes, sunrooms and solariums were spaces dedicated to enjoying sunlight or to growing plants; and they simply weren't used when temperatures were uncomfortable. Their value was enhanced by this sense of temporary availability—like spring strawberries or fall leaves they must be enjoyed in season.

The dining room of the house shown on the facing page, designed by George Homsey, is an expanded bay with the feel of a pavilion settled comfortably into its quiet forest setting. Surrounded by windows, it is intimately linked to the weather outside. Meals eaten here are elegant picnics, a departure from everyday mealtime routines.

The rectangular form of the bay window and the gable roof projected to cover it is repeated in various ways on different façades, becoming a theme of the Colorado house shown on p. 235.

This dining room uses natural materials, numerous windows, its location outside the walls of the main building, and its tentlike roof shape to emphasize the connection with the outdoors. Sitting here, surrounded by trees, is almost like being at a very comfortable campsite.

Looking through the garden gate of this home in the Hudson Valley, the gazebolike form of the summer room is visible projecting into the garden. The use of a shape associated with open structures contributes to the sense that this indoor room really is at home outdoors.

Like the dining room on the previous page, the summer room in a Hudson Valley home designed by Centerbrook Architects projects from the house and is almost entirely surrounded by windows. One of the characteristics of in-between places is that they are often difficult to define as either indoor or outdoor rooms. This summer room is uniquely able to play both roles. Built as an addition to an existing small house, it was designed to transport the owners out of their workaday city world into one of country comfort. The basic form of the original house is traditional and rectangular; so to create the sense of being in a space apart, the designers used a completely different geometry for the summer room. The almost octagonal space projects from the building and has a roof form that distinguishes it from the original house. It is surrounded on five sides by an herb garden—making it more a room in the garden than a room in the house.

In summer, the triple-hung windows are moved up, above door head height, leaving large screened openings below. The room then functions like a screened-in porch, open to breezes and filled with the scents of the garden. The choice of materials and the furnishings accentuate the sense of being outdoors—wicker chairs and slate floors belong to the exterior. In winter, fall, and spring the room takes on a more interior feel. Windows are closed, table lamps add warmth, and accessories belong to the realm of interior finishes. Yet the outdoors still surrounds the room; and a visit there captures the feeling of a trip to the garden.

A SUMMER ROOM

Set in a fragrant herb garden, this summer room protrudes from the building to gain a view to the pond below and to catch the breeze. When windows are open on all sides, cross-ventilation keeps the room cool.

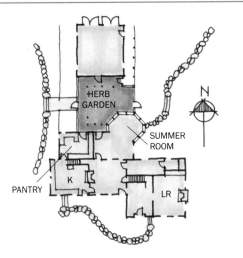

Make sure that interior places in between feel truly surrounded by the outdoors; otherwise they'll be just another room.

TOO SMALL TO BE A ROOM

To add to the quality of life, places in between do not need to be as generous as the summer room just described. Sometimes the most valuable quality of a space is its lack of an obvious assignable use. The sunroom attached to the south side of a Berkeley, California, home was too tiny (6 ft. by 8 ft. 6 in.) to even rate a mention on a real estate description, yet it was a determining factor in the owner's decision to purchase this house. Rational concerns about adequate storage and size or number of bedrooms can be overruled by the power of possibilities.

The south-facing sunroom with skylights, sliding wood-framed multipaned windows on three sides, and a view to the garden (see the drawing at right) conjured up visions of sewing in the morning sun, reading in the corner, or starting seedlings. That sunroom now serves as a studio, guest room, sewing room, office, and children's playroom. Too small to be a real room, it accommodates whatever activity suits the moment. With the French doors to the dining room open, the room connects to the house; when the doors are closed it is almost outside—a perfect in-between space.

A SOUTH-FACING SUNROOM *The sliding wood-framed windows in this tiny sunroom travel corner to corner and are right at desktop level; the lack of any sense of a wall behind the desk creates a strong connection to the outdoors.*

The side walls of this summer room are filled almost floor to ceiling with triple-hung windows. When the windows are fully open, the screens reach the head height of the doors, allowing the room to function as a screened-in porch. When the windows are closed, they offer full protection from cold or wet weather.

A House of Layers

WHILE SMALL PLACES IN BETWEEN can be almost magical in their ability to absorb a variety of activities, another sort of magic is possible when places in between are the organizing idea for a whole house. The Florida house we'll look at here, designed by Duany Plater Zyberk and Company, is all about being half in and half out. The house is on an island, facing the bay, and enjoys warm weather year round. The owners wanted a tropical house, not one of the bulked-up and closed villas that were filling the postage-stamp lots around them. They treasured the connection to weather, water, and surroundings possible in this climate and hoped for a home with an island feel, open and breezy. Although this house enjoys sunshine and terrific views, it is also exposed to hurricane weather and flooding. The trick

From the water, the house appears to be a solid form tucked under a Sheltering Roof; it is only as you move through the building that the play of in and out becomes clear.

A sturdy perimeter of concrete-block walls and roll-down shutters shelters the more fragile wood interior from hurricanes. The shutters provide security when fully closed and can be selectively positioned to offer shade.

was to create a house that was unusually open to the light, air, ventilation, and view offered by the location yet secure in the face of the storms that regularly travel up the coast.

BUILDING ON TRADITION

To meet this challenge, the architects drew on two local building traditions: frame and clapboard structures derived from the south Florida vernacular and concrete block and stucco from the current convention. Bowing to the need for protection from storms and to the closeness of neighboring homes, the designers planned sturdy concrete block perimeter walls along the side lines of the lot. With only a few small windows, the walls offer privacy and a strong structural frame for the house. A simple hipped roof forms a sturdy cap, a real SHELTERING ROOF, spanning between the block walls and presenting an almost conventional form to the street.

The walls facing the bay to the west and the street to the east are much more open, with a tall loggia forming a generous place in between the outer columns and the inner wall. The walls are transparent—a combination of windows and open-air passages (more places in between) that allow light to pass through. The major living areas are raised up one level above the ground, suspended between the side walls—a strategy that allows flood waters to pass beneath the house without harming it. The area below the house is used to park cars, while on the floor above, automatic roll-down shutters fill the large openings to secure the house against storms and provide security in the owners' absence.

ABOVE THE WEATHER
Placing the solid masonry walls perpendicular to the water and raising the floors above flood level allow the house to remain high and dry through storms.

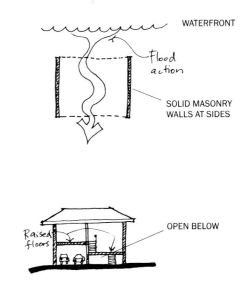

Filled with large plants and lightweight furniture, this large alcove off the living room is distinguished by exposed ceiling framing and walls of exterior siding reminiscent of porches.

Inside the shell formed by the side walls, a group of light wood-frame structures are clustered under the roof, linked by open passageways and stairs, surrounded by open decks and porches. The result is a tropical house freely arranged within the shelter of a block house—a house of layers in which places in between are the natural result of the design. The contrast between the dense solidity of the side walls and the airy openness of the space in between establishes a theme of linking solid and open that is carried on within the house, where light-filled alcoves hang off the sides of all the major rooms. The "serious" function of each room takes place in a conventional rectangular space with solid walls and very few small windows, while the alcove offers a bright place apart.

FOUR ALCOVES AND A LOGGIA

When the climate is mild and the setting attractive, it is important to create links to the outdoors throughout the house. Here, four alcoves create interior places in between off all the major rooms, while loggias and breezeways offer exterior settings with a wide variety of exposures.

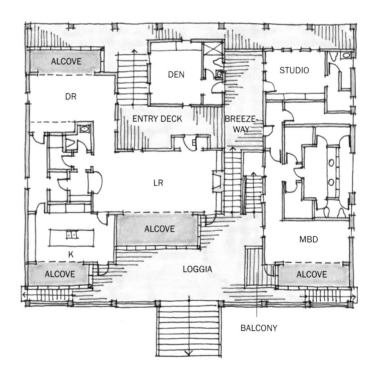

The eating alcove off the kitchen is bright and filled with light, yet it feels cozy in contrast to the high ceiling of the kitchen.

A PROTECTED BALCONY

Designing balconies that have qualities of being both inside and outside can be a challenge. Because balconies typically project from the wall, it can be difficult to achieve the sense of enclosure that invites real use. The balcony off the master bedroom at this house meets the challenge and is a real complement to the room it serves. The roof overhead contains the balcony within the framework of the building, while the view over the water creates an invitation to go outside. Overlooking the loggia below, the balcony becomes an important part of the intricate arrangement of spaces with varying levels of exposure and privacy that make up this island house.

This bedroom balcony offers a place to step outside and check the weather before dressing or to enjoy the evening view before going to bed. Because it is easy to access, it encourages the quick pauses that reconnect us with our surroundings.

COMPLEMENTARY ALCOVES

Ceilings throughout the house are high (over 13 ft.) with fans in the main rooms, which contribute to the tropical ambience. The alcoves at the perimeter are set apart by lower ceilings and by a framed and trimmed opening that marks the transition. The change in scale from room to alcove is an example of PARTS IN PROPORTION—each area is the right size for the activity that takes place there and creates a complementary space, which is enhanced by the contrast in size. Each of the four alcoves has a wall of windows on two sides but serves a different function, depending on the requirements of the room it joins. In the kitchen, the alcove is low, creating an intimate scale for an informal meal or a cup of coffee.

The dining room shown on the previous page is located on the north side of the building and has a darker and cooler feel at its center, while its alcove is a bright retreat looking into the trees. The alcove here has a high ceiling and really feels like an extension of the same room when furniture and lighting are used to join them. This works well to expand the apparent size of the dining room and accommodate additional tables and chairs for large events. On the other hand, the alcove can be treated as a space apart, a small sitting and display area, giving the dining room a smaller scale for regular use.

The living room alcove is the most generous, almost the size of a room. It works perfectly as a spot for one or two people to sit comfortably, a PRIVATE EDGE next to the COMMON CORE of the living room, safely outside the main flow of events. The final alcove lies just off the master bedroom, a sunny retreat from the darker interior and an indoor place in between.

LEFTOVER SPACES MAKE IN-BETWEEN PLACES

The rooms and alcoves of this island house are sandwiched between the block walls, then linked by the open spaces that remain under the sheltering roof. These spaces—loggia and breezeways—have both the casual quality of "leftover" spaces between buildings and the comfortable sense of enclosure felt on porches. The ambiguous nature of these areas is enhanced by the presence of the balcony and the open rails of the breezeways on the upper floor—also within the umbrella of the roof—that overlook the loggia below. Walking from the common areas of the house to the bedrooms requires leaving the climate-controlled interior for a trip through roofed but outdoor "halls"—a sure way to incorporate in-between moments of into everyday life.

Set beside the bay, this house creates the ambiance of a tropical vacation. The finishes are reminiscent of a beach cottage, the colors are bright and uninhibited in their application, the spaces are airy and light, and the outdoors is an essential element of the composition of spaces. In the sense that a vacation occurs in between the normal obligations of life to create a time of freedom, this house occurs in between the normal conventions of house design and creates a space that makes few demands and offers an array of possibilities.

Movement from room to room in this Florida house brings its residents onto protected loggias and breezeways, furnished to invite a pause to enjoy the weather and the view. Paddle fans ensure a breeze when the air is still.

The Flow through Rooms.
This island house is unique in that the most important passages are also places in between, areas of outdoor space that link indoor rooms ending in cul-de-sacs that serve as places to pause or linger. Traffic naturally flows along the edge of the cul-de-sacs on the exterior and along the edge of the common rooms on the interior.

Refuge and Outlook.
With its outlook across the bay from the refuge of the sheltered loggia, the house uses this pattern to organize its volume. Within the larger loggia, the balcony off the master bedroom offers refuge and outlook at a smaller scale.

Sheltering Roof.
The simple and encompassing form of the roof holds all of the smaller building pieces together. While ceilings are high to allow air circulation, the detail of the rafter tails and the deep overhang at the roof's edge create a sense of containment.

Parts in Proportion.
The large rectangular volume sheltered under the roof is broken into a series of similarly shaped spaces—elongated rectangles—that gradually decrease in size and height from rooms to alcoves. The same long rectangle is then used to divide the walls into glazed and solid areas and to shape the divided lights in windows and guardrails. Repetition of the form creates a sense of continuity and order, while the use of the same form in different dimensions and materials creates an intriguing complexity.

Warm Center, Cool Edges

At the opposite end of the climate spectrum from the island house, this year-round Maine home is located in an idyllic woodland setting. Winters in Maine can be long and harsh, and this home for all seasons needs to be comfortable throughout the year. The owner (who is the manager of Martinsville Vacation Rentals) wanted a house that fit into the mix of traditional cottages and more contemporary summer homes that surround the site. She asked for a house that would be flexible, suitable for spending time alone working in an office, but also capable of accommodating a variety of guests and friends.

This small home designed by John Silverio met all of her criteria and exceeded her hopes. The house is composed of very few rooms—the living areas and a master bedroom on the lower floor and a large activity area with a single guest room on the upper floor. Its sense of complexity, and the wide variety of experiences it offers, comes from developing the perimeter with places in between and from using contrast to give each space a unique character. The simple pyramidal forms of the SHELTERING ROOF create a strong sense of containment, which contrasts with the different spaces that cross the boundary from indoors to out.

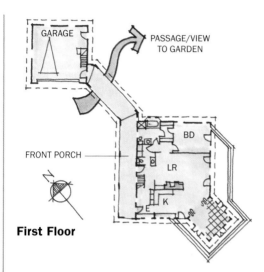

First Floor

The house is made up of two square forms joined by a steeply sloped roof that comes low on all sides and contains dormers on the upper floors—a Sheltering Roof that promises protection from the harsh Maine winters.

COOL EDGES

Places in between play a practical role in the life of houses. As porches or breezeways, they can capture outdoor space and claim it for the building. Easily accessed from inside, even in bad weather, they create a dry zone at the edge of building: a protected space for wood and tool storage, an area for removing wet or dirty boots and jackets, a place for sports equipment.

Surrounded on three sides by windows and large sliding doors, the sunroom is a particularly versatile space. Open to the light and the outdoors, the room can be a warm and inviting space when filled with sunlight and a cool porchlike retreat with the doors wide open. In very cold weather, thick velvet curtains can be drawn across the opening to keep the cool air out of the core.

On warm days, the breezeway linking house to garage lives up to its name, funneling the wind between the buildings to create a cool place for sitting and enjoying the garden.

The long entry porch protects the firewood in the cool months and provides welcome shade in summer.

This house begins with a classic half in, half out space: a long breezeway porch. Bridging the gap between the garage/studio building and the house, the breezeway creates a roofed car connection to the garage, offering protection from sun in summer and snow in winter. As you approach the house from the driveway, it frames a view into the back garden, simultaneously inviting further investigation and cautioning that the area beyond the breezeway is private.

Moving along the breezeway toward the front door, you make a turn and come under the low roof of the main building onto a linear front porch, which creates a sheltered entrance transition for the front door as well as convenient protected access into the kitchen. An example of THE FLOW THROUGH ROOMS, the porch travels along the edge of the outdoor rooms, uses light at the end of the porch to direct the flow, and provides interest along the passage. Broad enough to furnish, it is a comfortable outdoor room where you can sit, back against the building, and enjoy the day or come out on a snowy night and stay dry as you gather wood for the fireplace. Seen from outside, the deep shadows under the eaves at the breezeway and porch suggest the protection within; and the band of shade they produce not only creates comfortable sitting places for sunny days but shields interiors from heat gain and from the fading that results from direct sunlight.

WARM CENTER

In the Maine climate, any version of a pattern that seeks to balance in and out must be firmly anchored on the "in" side of the equation. The folk expression "When the house is strong, the storm is good" might here be amended to say, "When you have a warm center, it's good to spend time on the edge." The warm center is the comfortable all-purpose room at the geometric heart of the house. Anchored by its stately fireplace, this room is made to feel even more "inside" by the layer of spaces on the cool north side.

Placing the stair entry hall and support areas such as pantry, closets, and bathrooms on the north has a very real impact on the comfort of a house; the entire area forms a thermal buffer zone between the coldest wall and the interior. Separating this space with a framed door and transom window makes it clear that you have not really entered the heart of the house until you

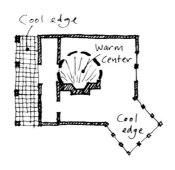

have crossed the threshold of the central room. The south-facing walls opposite are filled with windows to admit southern light and warmth, but they are also curtained to increase the sense of containment when the sun is not bright.

BETWEEN COOL AND WARM

In contrast to the warm center, the wide-open sunroom forms a cooler edge. Placed diagonally to the common areas, this room breaks out of the simple rectangular box of the plan and becomes a room full of

BETWEEN ROOF AND SKY

Dormer windows are at the opposite end of the scale from whole rooms that project out of the house. Literally popping out of the roof, dormers often feel almost like a separate structure—a small room added onto the room they adjoin.

Dormers serve two important practical functions. They bring light into a space that would otherwise be enclosed by the roof, and they increase the volume of space, projecting beyond the roof and increasing the amount of floor area with usable headroom. Because rooms that have dormers are shaped by the location of the windows within the roof, they typically have a very strong sense of being *in*—sloping walls and low ceiling heights create an almost womblike sense of enclosure (the warm center). The dormer offers a strong contrast—a sense of leaving the space of the room and moving *out,* beyond the roof, toward the outdoors, and the light (the cool edge).

The long view linking the seating area by the fire to the sunroom visually extends this small house, offering a chance to enjoy the extremes of warm and cool, light and dark in the space of a glance.

Located in the center of the house, this hard-working fireplace creates a strong sense of being in—enclosed in the center—a feeling that is enhanced by the interior transom window looking into a layer of rooms to the north.

light, open on three sides to the outdoors through large uncurtained doors and windows. Its eaves are narrow, allowing sun to penetrate deeply. With the sliding doors open, the wind can blow right through the room, and it is possible to walk outdoors to a floor-level deck on three edges. The simple fact of being at an angle to the other rooms gives this area the sense of being a place apart—intensifying the feeling of being half in, half out.

On the upper level there is a more modest version of the warm center and cool edge. Again, the colder north edge is filled with practical elements—closets and stairs fitted under the roof, with a recessed dormer at the top of the stairs creating a space for a window seat on the landing. At the warm center lies a multipurpose activity room, lit from above by a skylight at the peak of the roof. Two sides of the room have dormer windows reaching out to the light; the extra volume created by the dormers becomes a window seat alcove on one side and an office on the other, forming cool retreats at the edge.

In this Maine house, the play of contrasts gives the places in between their power. Linking warm with cold, out with in, light with dark, protected with exposed creates the possibility of a wide range of experiences. In this climate that can really dictate when and how space is used, the house responds with a design that allows users to choose their location along the thermal spectrum without losing their connection to the extremes.

Places in Between: The Essential Link

There is magic in places that fall between the inside and the outside—places where we can enjoy being exposed because we know comfort lies close at hand, places where we can relish being inside because we are fully aware of the storm outside. The spaces that offer these experiences can range in scale from small window seats to grand solariums and in enclosure from the contained feel of a dormer to the openness of a wide veranda. It is important for houses to shelter us from nature's storms, but it is also essential that they help us reconnect with nature's wonders. They do that by offering moments of being in between.

DUAL DORMERS *The Maine house features two versions of dormer windows. The recessed dormer is cut into the volume of the roof, which allows light to enter but does not add head height or increase usable floor space. The projected dormer pops out of the surface, increasing the total volume as well as bringing in light.*

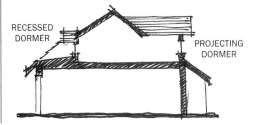

RECESSED DORMER

PROJECTING DORMER

On the cooler north side of the house, the dormer is recessed or inverted, suggesting that the spaces inside are secure deep within the roof. On the sunnier side, the dormers project, reaching out toward the light.

Contrast the various materials of construction, clarify the connections among them, and celebrate the innate qualities of each rather than covering them up.

COMPOSING WITH MATERIALS

This stair is a satisfying composition of wooden pieces that display their natural qualities, connections to each other, and contrast with the adjacent wall.

WHEN WE WROTE *A PATTERN LANGUAGE* IN 1977, we were struck by the empty feeling created by the materials of many modern buildings. Several of these materials—for example, exterior stucco and scored plywood wall surfaces, aluminum windows and doors, interior sheet goods such as plastic laminate and vinyl, and asphalt paving—began to deteriorate soon after installation. Attributing this to the materials themselves, we proposed the pattern Good Materials, which stated that more natural materials would ensure a more satisfying building, one that would continue to be beautiful over the years (provided that ongoing maintenance was part of the equation). Examples of these good materials included light-weight concrete, wood used sparingly, fabric coverings, ceramic tiles, and pervious gravel paving.

We have since somewhat modified our attitude toward building materials and try not to see the materials themselves as either good or bad. Instead, it's important to look more closely at how they are used in the design, how they relate to each other, and especially how they are allowed to display their innate qualities and characteristics. There are no good or bad materials—everything depends on how you use them.

Take, for example, the use of concrete and metal in the Campbell house interior (discussed later in this chapter). Both of these materials have unpleasant associations—concrete city sidewalks and metal cold to the touch. But when concrete is made into a richly colored and waxed floor slab or broken up into pieces to form stepping-stones

and low walls in the garden, the material begins to sing. Similarly, when all the various metal fittings in a room are unified and expressed in the same material, they become a synthesizing element, which helps tie the room together. In both cases, our attitude toward the material itself is transformed.

In this example, essential building materials have been transformed into objects of beauty by making them more visible and more expressive of their innate qualities. When the concrete floor slab is exposed, colored, and polished, we start to see it in a new light and are more appreciative of its true nature. And when the various metal fixtures are orchestrated to share the same metal and finish, we begin to see them as a continuous thread of decorative touches.

WORKING WITH THE PATTERN

Putting materials together in a way that promotes their longevity and visibility is the art of Composing with Materials. The key is to expose and clarify the materials of construction, letting each express its purpose and inner nature.

Concrete is not normally thought of as a desirable residential material, but in this entry it is effectively used as a richly colored waxed floor and, in a related form, as structural columns of concrete block. Similarly, silvery metal becomes an important material accent when used appropriately and consistently in bolts, outlet covers, hardware, and stair railings.

◢ *Emphasize the properties of materials* by placing them next to materials of contrasting texture or color. For example, contrast rough beams with creamy smooth walls, periodically insert contrasting tiles or dividing strips into the grid of concrete, and alternate bands of rough and smooth masonry.

◢ *Use different colors and textures* for different components of the building. Contrast roof and wall materials, and wall materials with trim and sash.

◢ *Emphasize the beginnings and endings* of individual parts. The exposed end of a piece of wood, for example, demands special attention. The individual logs in a rustic cabin might show an end finished with an ax, while the end of a piece of cabinetry might be finished with a miter saw, file, and sandpaper.

- *Clarify the connections* between the parts of the building. The visible connectors of the different building elements—such as screws, metal plates, bolts, washers, flashings—should be emphasized to explain the transfer of forces or change in materials.

- *Contrast the beauty* of raw, naturally occurring wood and rocks with the qualities of worked and refined materials (such as engineered wood or corrugated metal and plastic). Each has aesthetic potential when used directly and combined carefully.

- *When a material has the potential to achieve an attractive patina of age,* don't obscure the process, even with a protective coating. Wood shingles, for example, burnish to a dark color in the sun or take on a greenish moss color in the shade and have a beauty of their own, which is integral to the material. It is that quality of the material that should be celebrated in the building. While paint (or opaque stain) might protect the shingles, it covers up their innate beauty and must be reapplied many times before the shingles need to be replaced.

- *Where you choose a material or finish that ages quickly,* like painted wood or canvas awning, commit to a program of periodic maintenance. The occasional renewal will produce a sparkling, fresh feeling to the building.

- *Materials used in a new way* can heighten our appreciation of them. Examples are exterior materials used inside (wood shingles, corrugated fiberglass or metal, brick) or interior materials used outside (furniture on a covered porch, fabric awnings).

Bathrooms offer a great opportunity for creating a harmonious assembly of materials. This one by George Homsey shows fresh approaches to the countertop, sink, cabinet, and door handles, using honesty, exposure, and simplification to celebrate the inner nature of the materials.

This house is an enclosed compound, protected by the entry gatehouse and by the 18-in.-thick soil/cement buildings and surrounding walls. The other major materials here are the red clay tile roofing and the green-painted wood of the window shutters.

The dry, warm earthen walls are the perfect foil for the water of the pool and the coolness of the plantings. The walls contrast in terms of smoothness, solidity, warmth, and color, intensifying the effect of all the materials.

BUILT FROM THE EARTH

Earth has been used as a building material for millennia, but in recent years there has been renewed interest in this material because of its aesthetic and ecological potential. David Easton and his wife, Cynthia Wright, designed and built their own house in Napa, California, using "rammed earth" for the garden walls (a technique in which a soil and cement mixture is tamped down solidly in between wall forms) and a new approach for the structural walls (whereby a soil and cement slurry is pneumatically blown onto a grid of steel rebar held in position by plywood forms). The inspiration for the house came from materials and details used in Mediterranean houses—specifically, thick walls built of materials from the earth (then sometimes stuccoed or plastered), smallish windows, sparing use of wood, and integration of landscape and house.

Their design has taken the shape of an enclosed courtyard, formed by the earthen walls of both the buildings and the connecting enclosure walls. The various functions are broken into separate buildings to create a villagelike assembly of structures. From the outside, the home seems like a town that you enter through a protecting gatehouse.

BACKGROUND MATERIALS

The major materials are clearly announced at the entry gatehouse: smooth peach-pink earthen walls, rough-textured red clay roofing tile, sparing use of wood for dark green–painted shutters and doors, and pale green–painted metal windows. What's so pleasing about this assembly of materials is that each one gets a chance to shine, to present itself against a contrasting background. The pink earthen walls flow on and on, uninterrupted, acting as a background for the more highly textured and colored clay tiles and painted shutters. The simple plain walls also constitute a wonderful background for the rich greenery of the plantings.

The inner courtyard repeats all these material themes but adds an important new element—the water of the pool and wall fountain beyond. The water is welcome in the dry Mediterranean-like climate, contrasting sharply with the warm, sun-baked earthen walls. The success of this particular assembly of materials can be emphasized by imagining the same buildings and spaces in different materials—say wood planked walls and fences with composition shingle roofs. The buildings would not be as solid, as firmly connected to earth, and would not provide as strong a framework for the pool and landscaping.

Contrast is also used in some of the smaller exterior details. An outdoor sitting area is provided on solid paving up against the strong earthen walls but then covered with a very delicate, semitransparent overhead grape arbor built from recycled 2-in.-diameter well casings. The solid elements work well in conjunction with the delicate ones, each contributing to the vividness of the other. The resulting outdoor room is comfortable because the grape leaves shade the users (and the wall of the building) in the summer but fall off in the winter to allow full winter sun (see CREATING ROOMS, OUTSIDE AND IN).

The apparent strength and solidity of the earthen walls is intensified by the open delicateness of the overhead grape trellis.

THE MATERIALS CONTINUE INSIDE

The house is linked to the exterior not only by generous French doors but also by the presence of the earthen walls that continue into the interiors. The massiveness of the wall material is emphasized by the arched shape of the entry doorway. The beefy exposed wooden ceiling beams were recycled from an Oakland port and left in their original rough and rustic finish to express their utilitarian character and their role of holding up a second floor. The floor, paved in substantial and durable site-built soil and cement tiles, is more smoothly finished and waxed, to give a luxurious feel and to contrast sharply with the rough beams above.

The thickness of walls becomes particularly apparent at the window openings, further emphasized by a frame of individual soil and cement surround blocks. The cement ratio of these blocks was increased to produce a denser, stronger material, reinforcing the opening and highlighting it with a special pattern and lighter color.

The house is an eloquent statement of how materials—mainly soil and cement with secondary themes of roof tile, wood beams, and painted wood doors and windows—can be composed to complement each other and displayed to demonstrate their innate beauty.

RUSTIC AND REFINED

One way of uniting a house to its landscape is to build it out of the materials of the site itself. In the house we just looked at, earth was used to build walls. In the next house, some of the wood from the trees of the mountains is incorporated into the building. But the rugged site and these raw materials are then contrasted with careful detailing and fine workmanship.

This family compound in the high Sierras of California consists of three separate buildings, partly connected via covered outdoor walks.

The window openings are thickened with individual surround blocks, also made with a soil and cement mixture. Simply removing a little of the thick wall and inserting a shelf or two creates interesting areas for display.

The rammed-earth walls also appear in the interiors, where they are joined by rustic wooden ceiling beams and waxed concrete floor tiles.

The materials of the site—wood and rock—are refined and elegantly put together in the house. As a result, both the site and the house are more beautiful together than either could be alone.

Contrast the beauty of raw, naturally occurring wood and rocks with the qualities of worked and refined materials.

The clustering of separate buildings gives the appearance of a small mountain mining or logging town. Knitted into and between the huge boulders of the sloping site, the clean, utilitarian sheds of the buildings are sheathed in vertical cedar boards and battens and roofed with corrugated galvanized iron. These materials help make the site itself more dramatic and beautiful by contrasting the coolness of the gray granite rocks with the warmth of the wood color and repeating their tones in the coolness of the gray roof.

One of architect George Homsey's strategies for ennobling materials is to contrast the rustic with the refined. As an example, take a look at the building in the top photo on the facing page. The raw red-fir tree trunks from the site that support the porch overhang stand in strong contrast to the more refined sawn wood boards and battens of the wall skin. There is something arresting about the economy of the thin wood sheathing next to the luxury of the generously oversize tree trunks. At a lower scale of detail, the rough-sawn board-and-batten siding is integrated with the painted wood-framed windows to permit some batts not only to seal the joint between two boards but also to constitute the jamb trim of the window. Rough materials, elegant details.

Through elegant detailing and the elimination of all unnecessary elements, the wood is allowed to generate a quiet glow of beauty.

RESPECT FOR MATERIALS IN EXTERIOR DETAILING

Architects use the term *detailing* to describe the small-scale relationships between building parts, such as where a roof meets a wall. Architect George Homsey is a master of effective and clear detailing, and there are a couple of signature details in this house. One is the concrete foundation top, which is brought up well clear of the ground to keep the wood dry and termite free but then carefully detailed to produce an elegant base to the house. Its top edge is chamfered, or angled, to shed water away from the bottom ends of the siding. This simple gesture helps transform the practical necessity of a concrete foundation into an object of beauty.

Our appreciation of materials is heightened by contrasting large scale with small and contrasting roughness with very careful detailing for economy, elegance, and long life.

ROUGH AND SMOOTH INTERIORS

The interiors continue the theme of contrast between rustic and refined. The bedroom walls and ceilings are sheathed with knotty pine boards, a material with a vigorous grain and surface pattern. This texture is balanced with the economy of the detailing—boards that butt tightly to one another, not only along their length but also at their ends where the wall meets the ceiling. And these boards themselves form the window and door trim, doubling their function and vastly simplifying the finished appearance and feeling of the room (though demanding much more craftsmanship from the builders). The result is a quiet, almost reverential mood, allowing the wood to express its own inherent beauty.

But materials can also express a sense of fun and joy. In the hallway, fallen trees from the site were de-barked and assembled together to form the guardrail. This is a nice example of form fitting the function, where the machined boards are used to cover the flat wall framing, and the natural pole forms are used for the individual balusters. The mixing of humankind's and nature's craftsmanship heightens our appreciation for both.

Can materials express a sense of humor? These natural balusters from fallen tree trunks on the site create a delightful balance to the refined detailing and construction of the walls.

Small House, Beautiful Materials

WHEN HOWARD DAVIS DECIDED TO BUILD A HOUSE for himself in Eugene, Oregon, his budget constraints led him to economize on the size of the site, the overall size of the house, and the simplicity of its design. But he refused to scrimp on materials. As an architect, he knew that he could squeeze a lot of usefulness out of a limited amount of ground and square footage, but he also understood that the beauty of materials, carefully chosen, would enrich the experience of the house.

The exterior appearance of the 1,200-sq.-ft. house is modest and straightforward. From the street, a simple front porch is covered with a shed roof, but given more prominence by the presence of an intersecting gable roof just above. In Oregon, a land of cedar trees, Davis chose to sheathe not only the walls in cedar shingles but also the roof. The result is a little furry bear of a house, a cottage. This could have led to a rather monotone appearance, but Davis contrasted the shingles with the cool blue-green paint of the window, door, and rafter trim, a color that is complementary to the rich, warm, reddish and brown hues of the shingles.

And Davis had a couple of tricks up his sleeve. First, he added special punch and excitement to the entry by treating the front door to a bright yellow paint job, with sympathetic echoes in the three inset ceramic tiles just above it (we'll see a repeat of the yellow tiles inside the house). Next, Davis embellished the entry by using smooth, tightly fitted wooden boards for the porch roof, railing material, and bench—an echo of the fine paneling and wainscoting found inside.

The large central room is surrounded by subsidiary spaces that are as small as practical and as open to the main space as possible (an example of the pattern PRIVATE EDGES, COMMON CORE). The

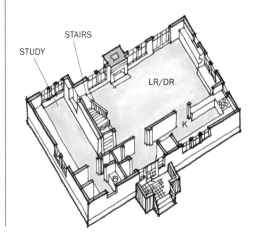

A SIMPLE PLAN *The modest plan can be thought of as a great room enriched by surrounding support spaces.*

This simple exterior has a powerful entry. It is centered and given further importance by the gable roof directly above it. And it is dressed up with a yellow door and three inset yellow tiles above.

Unpainted wood draws attention to the innate qualities of the material itself. Painted wood shelving can recede and allow the displayed objects to shine.

The large central living/dining room, a simple rectangle in plan, is enriched by small surrounding spaces—the study through the glass door, the stairs, and the partly open kitchen from which you can see the whole room.

kitchen is tiny but open to the main room, and the study is compressed but looks back into the living room through its entry and interior window. Even the stairs are kept open to the central large space, thereby adding to its visual generousness.

CONTRAST AND LINK

The material theme of the interior begins with the floors of patterned oak strip flooring, which are left a natural color. This continuous, uninterrupted floor plane is partnered on the first floor with a wooden ceiling of exposed Douglas fir floor joists and clear Douglas fir ceiling boards. Connecting these two horizontal surfaces are the walls of smooth drywall, painted an even, sunny, light yellow. We appreciate

REFRESHMENT FOR THE EYE

Just like our taste buds, our eyes require visual palate cleansers. In a room filled with such a fullness of warm yellow-orange-red-browns, there's a danger that our eyes will become fatigued. But here, the contrasting cool blues and greens that do appear (the blue cushion of the built-in bench, the green in the vases and plants, and especially the varied green ceramic tiles of the fireplace) take on a special power and balancing intensity. They provide just what the doctor ordered—an injection of a contrasting color as a refreshment for the eye.

The architect further refines this effect with four yellow tiles that link the fireplace back to the surrounding woods (reminding us of the three tiles above the exterior of the front door). In this warmly colored room, the touches of neutral black and white—the photos and their frames, the occasional bowl or plate, and table—are very striking. The effect would be equally noticeable in a uniformly cool-spectrum room.

the raw beauty of the natural wood floor and ceiling precisely because they contrast with the plain, creamy smooth, textureless walls that connect them.

Strong contrast—such as between wood and drywall—can be refined by linking the materials to each other in some way for a more integrated, richer, complex composition. In this room, Davis has linked the walls to the wood floor and ceiling by running wood wainscoting around the perimeter of the room. Breaking out of this wainscoting are the door and window trim, built-in seats, cabinets, and shelving all of the same Douglas fir as the overhead beams and ceiling, but closer in smoothness to the drywall.

*Emphasize the properties of materials
by placing them next to materials of
contrasting texture or color.*

TO PAINT OR NOT TO PAINT?

Painted woodwork is forgiving because the woodwork can be caulked before painting. And paint enables the woodwork to be either emphasized or not. The upper wall cabinets in the dining area, for example, are painted to almost match the walls and thus recede. They say less, so that their contents—the variously colored books and display objects—can say more (see the photo on p. 262).

In the same room, the unpainted wall paneling and Douglas fir trim stand cleanly on the wall for us to appreciate. Natural wood demands careful craftsmanship because here we see every cut, finish nail, and joint. When it is done well, we can move beyond appreciation of the finish carpenter's work and start to perceive the beauty of the raw material itself.

COLOR IN THE KITCHEN

Kitchens are interesting rooms in terms of materials and colors, because the appliances themselves take on such an important role. Affordable appliances tend to come in white with stainless-steel and

The kitchen repeats the warm-spectrum color scheme of the main living/dining room, but in a more intense form, with whiter white, redder red, and so on. All this warmth beautifully sets off the cooler-colored plants outdoors.

While the light walls are in strong contrast to the wood floors and ceiling, the wainscoting, cabinets, and shelving tie them back together, creating a harmonious result.

black details, and the designer is faced with the job of integrating them into a harmonious overall color and material scheme.

Davis has succeeded here by continuing the white of the appliances in the tiled backsplash, sink, and lower cabinet pulls. From this starting point, colors are picked up from the whole warm spectrum of the large central room and repeated in deeper, more intense tones—yellow lower cabinets, orange counter tile, dark orange-red upper cabinets, upper wall paneling, and ceiling. Again, with such a warm-spectrum color ensemble, touches of complementary green in the crockery, pictures, and vegetables—and especially in the trees outside the kitchen window—take on tremendous power and intensity. The colors of the large central room are enriched by appearing in a more intense form in the smaller surrounding study and kitchen. This is similar to the detailed design of traditional Asian carpets, in which each area of color is edged by a boundary of more intense color.

The upstairs ceilings follow the shape of the roof above, increasing the feeling of being inside. The library is open to the main area, preserving a sense of spaciousness.

THE WARMTH OF ENCLOSING MATERIALS

Upstairs, materials are slightly less formal, with knotty pine instead of clear Douglas fir for the ceiling, which is raised to follow the bottom of the roof trusses. Overall, this creates a comforting, enclosed feeling, almost as if you were in a wooden boat. The vigor of the knotty pine ceiling boards is intensified by the lack of trim where they touch the drywall.

At the back of the house, the upstairs balcony is like a birdhouse, providing shelter within the volume of the house and permitting a safe, secure vantage point from which to oversee the activity and garden below (REFUGE AND OUTLOOK). The way the materials are assembled is also key to its success. The surrounding warm wood of the interior is repeated at the balcony, preserving the sense that you are still partly indoors, still part of the house. And the softened, angled corners of the opening add to the gentleness of the space's embrace.

Repeating similar wood paneling on the exterior walls of the upstairs balcony reinforces its link with the interior of the house.

A House Whose Structure Is Also Its Finish

CRAIG AND SHARON CAMPBELL worked with the Seattle architectural firm of Miller/Hull on a house that's full of interesting ideas about the use of materials. Their house is a good example of starting with affordable and durable materials, and then combining them in a way that allows their inherent beauty to emerge. The result is a disciplined but elegant little house set into the harsh but beautiful landscape of eastern Washington.

The site plan shows a flat orchard bordered on the east by a hill, which separates the orchard from a view to the east and falls away for many miles. The house was carved into the back of this hill to gain the view, shelter from the predominant west winds, and the anchor of a magnificent Ponderosa pine. The entry to the house is protected by a rolling gate that normally stays shut to shield the inner court from the wind.

THE MESSAGE OF MATERIALS

From the introductory views of the house, the broad material themes of its construction announce themselves: almost flat zinc-aluminum roofs on fully exposed 4×6 rafters, partly supported by wooden walls and partly by steel frames, and a base of unapologetic standard concrete block. From the entry, this appears to be a tough little building designed to withstand rough weather and provide uncompromising security for its residents.

Once through the entry gate, it's clear that this is only half the story. The sheltering concrete block on the west side of the building gives way to delicate wood and glass walls on the eastern view side that can be opened up in good weather for outdoor living.

In this south view of the house, all the themes of the materials are brought together and restated—the contrast between rough and smooth, natural and man-made, concrete shear walls and steel load-bearing beams, exposed connections, solidity and transparency.

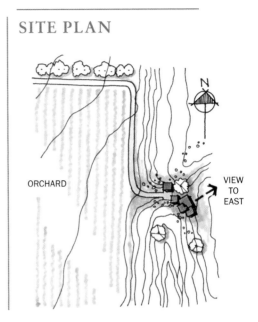

SITE PLAN

ORCHARD

VIEW TO EAST

The rolling entry gate provides security and creates a more sheltered climate for the inner court. It opens to reveal a spectacular view beyond.

Once through the entry gate, the guarded exterior on the east changes to warmer and more delicate materials.

This entry sequence illustrates the notion that materials carry messages, associations that the architect can manipulate to underscore the overall design concept. The heavy, no-nonsense concrete block tells us that we are on the exterior public side of the house, while the lighter, more delicate wood and glass announce the interior private side. In a further refinement of this idea, the block wall is used to create a transition between the public part of the patio and the private part that serves the master bedroom. The block wall that forms the division between the kitchen and the master bedroom is extended out beyond the building to form a symbolic gateway, guarding the private portion of the patio.

The materials also express structural messages. The architects put the structure in plain view so that we can understand how the materials work. The heavy concrete block is below, visibly supporting the lighter wood-framed walls and roof above. The steel beams, with their twin splayed pipe column supports, clearly hold up the ends of the roof extensions, and visible metal clips connect the roof rafters to these steel beams. All the details of construction of the sliding wood and glass doors are exposed, helping us understand how the building is put together.

Finally, the plan shows how the sturdy concrete block retaining walls (colored gray) permit the house to be dug into the solid hill at its back, while the thinner wood and glass walls on the east perimeter allow good views for all the living spaces. This material language of "back" and "front" is underscored by the placement of stairs, bath, and utility room on the back side to permit unobstructed views for the living spaces.

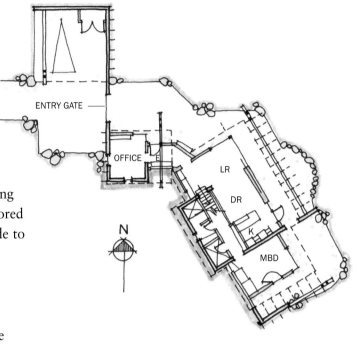

BLURRING THE DISTINCTION BETWEEN OUTSIDE AND IN

As you enter the living room, it quickly becomes obvious that the themes of the exterior material composition are repeated on the interior. The colored concrete floors of the patio continue right inside, forming the finished interior floor, and are heated by circulating hot water. The common concrete block walls continue inside as well, accompanied by the oiled steel beams and metal connectors, the structural roof beams (recycled from an older building), and planking. Simply put, there is no difference between exterior materials and interior materials. Except for occasional areas of interior wood cabinetry, the materials of the house do not change character as they come into the house, do not soften or become more refined. The effect of this is to intermix interior and exterior living experience, strengthening the feeling that the house is an integral part of nature, not a just a retreat from it.

Similarly, there is no distinction between structure and finish materials as in a more conventional house. Here the structure *is* the finish. The materials themselves are very satisfying, and finishes in this house would only detract from the aesthetic pleasures they offer. This attitude even extends to the mechanical systems. In the bathroom, the exposed wall-mounted radiant heating register (just visible in the mir-

The privacy of the master bedroom patio is marked by the concrete block wall that extends out from the kitchen, forming a gateway.

The exterior concrete paving and block walls are repeated on the interior directly, without apology.

The unadorned and raw materials of concrete block, concrete countertop, and colored concrete floor are tempered by the warmth of the wood cabinet. Towels are warmed by the exposed wall-mounted radiant heater.

SPECIAL EFFECTS

Materials can be manipulated to produce a special effect, as in the kitchen cabinetry shown here, a project mainly tackled by Sharon Campbell herself, with help from metal artist Carl Dern. Sharon detailed the cabinets from clear Douglas fir but covered those closest to the stove and hood with acid-washed steel panels whose colors were inspired by the surrounding natural site. These doors are opened via ornate steel handles shaped to resemble snakes. The central bull's-eye image was painted onto the hood using acrylics.

The technique of mixing rough and elegant materials is used here in the contrast between the concrete floor and block wall and the finely finished smooth cabinetry. This contrast is heightened further by the exquisite minor details of the cabinetry—a sloping base for a larger work surface, the integral knife slot, and the cleanly raised dining counter. Similarly, the various

Materials can be inventively worked and manipulated to create new effects, as in these acid-washed metal panel doors and stove hood.

shades of stained resawn wood that make up the different areas of wood walls were based on the native and surrounding plant colors—the cool green of sage brush and lichen, the yellow of poplar leaves, and the deep red of the native grasses.

ror in the photo at left on the facing page) adds to our understanding of how the house is heated and offers the added benefit of warming the bath towels.

The Campbell house, which stakes a claim in a tough dry climate, incorporates and celebrates tough materials of concrete and steel. Yet, the final result has warmth, dignity, even sensuality. Heat is provided where it will give the greatest comfort (in the floor), and wood is used either where it is the most economical structural material (the roof rafters and planking) or where our hands will feel its warmth to the touch (the cabinetry). The materials of the house take care of the deepest needs of the people who live there.

The Joy of Building

Materials used in a new way can heighten our appreciation of them.

IN THE PREVIOUS HOUSE, we talked about using materials in terms of structure—load-bearing beams, posts, and walls, with attention to resistance to lateral force—all very serious stuff. But materials can also be used expressively, for emphasis, for sensual pleasure, or playfully, with a sense of humor. This house by Richard Fernau and Laura Hartman for a dramatist, a writer, and their small child is an example of materials being composed in a lighter spirit, full of surprises. This house awakens a new appreciation of materials, showing that they can speak not only quietly and subtly but also boldly, dramatically, and freshly.

The northern California site is magnificent, with an extraordinary view over the hills to a reservoir beyond and below. In this spectacular open land, it's best if the exterior of this house doesn't try to upstage the site. The exterior of this house is energetic and playful in its informal assembly of rectangular shapes, strung out along and across the contour, each sporting its own roof. But in another sense, the exterior is understated, the wall and roof colors a muted green and gray, the forms broken down into smaller and less domineering pieces. In this, it's reminiscent of a rural agricultural complex, with central barn, attached accessory sheds, and smaller detached buildings, all working together somehow purposefully, but a little mysteriously too.

The plan shows the informal placement of the parts, with the entry road parallel to the contours, past a future pool complex on the right, with guest parking and office on the left, to the garage straight ahead. It also hints that this house is going to have some surprises inside, with rooms that seemingly embed themselves into the body of the main space at unusual angles.

The house does not try to command the site; it is understated, fitting in modestly and informally.

AN INFORMAL PLAN

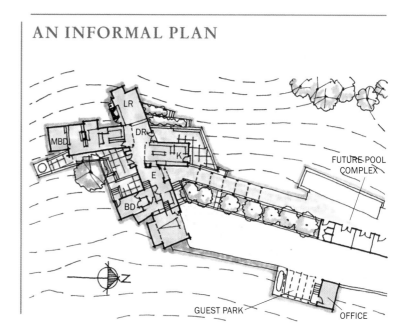

The first glimpse of the living room from the entry reveals a mysterious protrusion of elements into an otherwise pristine arched ceiling.

The surprise of the unusually bold color on the metal garage door is a reminder of the aesthetic potential of often-mundane elements.

THE RED GARAGE

The house gives an initial impression of informality and casualness. The driveway points to the garage directly ahead, but the rest of the house is shielded from view by plantings and a trellis. The first surprise is the red metal garage door—an isolated bold color among subdued surrounding colors of site, exterior walls, and landscaping. A visitor might ask, "Is this a joke? Red is a great color, but is it okay to paint a garage door that boldly?" The answer is yes, it is not only okay but a good lesson in converting an object that is usually hidden and deemphasized into an opportunity for appreciation. It is almost impossible to pass by this door without touching it to absorb some of its richness and warmth.

The dug-in guest parking area to the left presents the next material lesson. The concrete retaining wall, raw wood structural framing, and metal attachment plates all suggest industrial building. But the overall high quality of craftsmanship takes these materials to a new level of appreciation. Nothing has been left to chance, with every joint and connection carefully detailed, resulting in a renewed respect for the building. A similar attention to detail can be seen in the elegant stair that leads up to an office studio space; it has warm-colored wooden treads contrasted with cool perforated metal risers, an unusual combination that enhances both mate-

STEPPING DOWN THE SITE

Downhill Side   **Uphill Side**

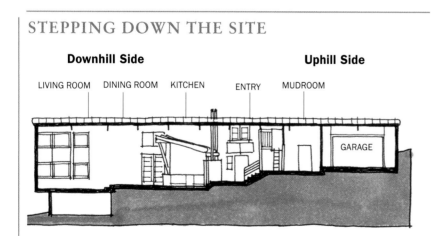

LIVING ROOM   DINING ROOM   KITCHEN   ENTRY   MUDROOM   GARAGE

The drama of the kitchen derives from the overhead trellis, the brilliantly colored linoleum flooring and Fin-Ply cabinet doors, the sparkle of the stainless-steel appliances, and the promise of a glowing fire.

rials (see the top photo on p. 280). And the refined wooden wall boards of the studio contrast strikingly with the overall industrial palette of the rest of the parking structure.

MATERIALS AT THE ENTRY

The entry is a half level down from the garage and child's bedroom. It is announced on the exterior by a natural Alaskan cedar post on a carefully detailed concrete base (see the top left photo on p. 278). This post is not required structurally, but it was placed to highlight, through contrast with the stained wood of the exterior, the singular importance of the front door.

A detached cedar post and concrete base add interesting detail and importance to the front-door alcove.

The materials in the entry include a colored concrete floor, blond Fin-Ply walls, and touches of galvanized sheet metal in the chimney flue and storage cubbies above the bench.

The materials present various dimensions of contrast—hard and soft, warm and cool, exterior and interior. The resulting entry room is vivid, playful, and inviting.

Immediately inside the entry, a bench for changing shoes is topped with cabinets and galvanized sheet-metal baskets with storage for each family member. The major wall material here and in the rest of the house is a refined type of dense and smooth prestained plywood called Fin-Ply. The panels are screwed onto the walls with narrow open joints between panels and the ceiling. This plywood is so dense that, unlike conventional plywood, the cut edge retains its integrity and can be exposed, as in its use as window trim.

The entry combines exterior and interior materials—hard and soft, fabricated and natural. The metal railing up to the garage and secondary bedroom is reminiscent of an exterior deck railing, and the wood siding of the exterior is brought into the entry, with a natural finish instead of transparent stain. The metal doors and frames contrast with the natural wood of the steps up to the bedroom, just as the polished concrete floor contrasts with the Fin-Ply of the adjacent walls. All of these various contrasting materials tend to make each of the separate elements—doors, stairs, floor, railing, walls—stand out as a separate entity. The units of function are assembled, like Tinker Toys, into colorful and interesting combinations.

MORE SURPRISES

From the entry, a ladder leads up to a bonus space above the front door, a tiny secret "roomlet." It works as a hideaway, almost like an indoor tree house, from which kids can look down and spy on the action below. As you leave the entry and move toward the kitchen and living space, the next surprise reveals itself. Ahead and above lie the great curved glulam beams of the main space that support a wood-planked ceiling. But this bold and direct design element appears to be only the container of other more complex forms jutting into the main

space—a jaunty little porch roof on one side and some mysterious ceiling framing entering the space from the other (see the photo on p. 274).

But turning the corner and looking into the open kitchen, it's revealed that the roof form of the exterior part of the kitchen wing is simply carried on into and under the main volume. This redundant continuation of roof framing forms a kind of overhead trellis for the part of the kitchen that lies inside the main space (see the plan on p. 275). This dramatizes the kitchen space and creates the feeling that it is a kind of stage set for a cooking performance. The kitchen glows with the intensity of the red linoleum floor, sparkling stainless-steel appliances, and red-stained Fin-Ply cabinet door panels. The marble-dust finish of the stucco fireplace and concrete hearth provides further

In addition to Composing with Materials, the commons space at the heart of the home incorporates at least five other patterns: Private Edges, Common Core; Capturing Light; Refuge and Outlook; Sheltering Roof; and Places in Between.

The warm wood stair treads contrast elegantly with the cool perforated metal risers, enhancing both.

Through omission of the unnecessary and distracting, this bathroom has a calm focus on the essential sink, lights, and mirror.

impact. All of these strong colors, textures, and details of the kitchen combine to bring life to the larger, simpler commons space, just as we saw earlier in the Davis house.

A MIX OF MOODS

The house offers not only excitement and a sense of fun but also a measure of quiet, elegance, and peacefulness. In contrast to the kitchen, the living room offers calmer expanses of plywood walls and the familiar comfort of overstuffed chairs. This room is elegant and modern, rich in materials but otherwise unornamented. The restful window seat is treated as a separate room with its own unique roof framing, ceiling, and wall paneling, all to emphasize its "outdoor" character. Compare this with the balcony in the Davis house, which was made to feel more interior by the use of interior wall treatment (see the bottom photo on p. 267).

The house is full of smaller details that further illustrate the thoughtful, sensitive use of materials, resulting in an almost meditative feeling. The bathrooms, for example, are unusually calm because of what is omitted. Examples include a minimum of cabinet doors, reuse of the same natural ply walls instead of tile, a simple slab of green slate countertop rather than highly figured granite or tile, and a tiny tile floor pattern—so tiny that it becomes a uniform texture. This simplification permits more careful attention to what remains: softly diffused light from two sides to avoid shadows and an unusual sparkle in the galvanized sheet-metal medicine cabinet that reminds us to look again at the inherent beauty in a material that we usually associate with heating ducts and gutters. The ribbed glass in the door lets in light from outside while maintaining privacy.

One final small detail that illustrates how the novel use of materials can bring delight and a fresh mood to a room is the use of chalkboard as wainscoting in the child's bedroom (see the photo on the facing page). Instead of telling kids not to draw on the walls, why not give them a wall designed for that purpose? The chalkboard's cool green color works as a complement to the brighter warm paint colors of the room's furniture, bringing a deep sense of completeness to the room.

The Potential Magic of Materials

Each of the houses described for this pattern is composed of a different palette of materials. What binds them together is the remarkable skill with which their designers have transformed the materials at hand into something magical. The lesson learned from these examples, above all, is to assemble materials in a way that respects their individual qualities.

By *respect for materials*, we mean that they are selected not only for their strength, durability, and affordability but also with openness to their unique aesthetic and emotional possibilities. It means that we should clarify, not hide, the joints and connections between them to show how they are assembled and should clarify the differences between materials to heighten their uniqueness. In the end, what we hope is that the people who live in the house will look at the everyday materials that surround them in a fresh way and exclaim, "Wow, I never realized how beautiful that could be!"

We have described this house in terms of Composing with Materials, but it also is a good example of several other patterns, which are summarized here and illustrated in the main living room.

Private Edges, Common Core. The "porch roof" over the seating area at the right edge of the commons helps define an area that is part of the commons but is slightly set off.

Capturing Light. Its translucent roofing tempers the light from a higher skylight and permits some to reach the master closet via an interior window—an unusual example of this pattern.

Refuge and Outlook. The ceiling rafters over the kitchen area obscure the view of someone in the roomlet over the entry door who is looking down into the commons from this secret vantage point.

Sheltering Roof. The main curved barrel-roof ceiling and the subsidiary interior porch and kitchen roofs are interior nested versions of this pattern.

Place in Between. Just around the corner of the kitchen is a breakfast nook, full of light on two sides, that is between the inside of the kitchen and the vast outdoors beyond.

Materials—in this case, the wainscotting in the child's bedroom—can be rethought and selected on the basis of real use, color, or even novelty, all to refresh our awareness of their inner beauty.

CREDITS

pp. ii and 256–259: DAVID EASTON, RAMMED EARTH WORKS (101 S. Coombs St., Studio N, Napa, CA 94559; 707-224-2532)

pp. v, 31, and 32: THE JOHNSON PARTNERSHIP, Larry Johnson, Principal in Charge, and Jill Sousa, Project Architect (1212 N. 65th St., Seattle, WA 98115; 206-523-1618; www.thejohnsonpartnership.com)

pp. vi, 4–5 (bottom), 7, 253, and 262–267: HOWARD DAVIS (541-342-6247; hpdavis@ixnetcom.com)

pp. 1 (top), 16 (left), 27, 28, 104, 105, and 215–223: THOMAS L. BOSWORTH FAIA, Bosworth Studio (1408 N. 45th St., Seattle, WA 98103; 206-545-8434; www.thebosworthstudio.com)

pp. 1 (bottom left, bottom right), 12 (top right), 74, 75, and 80–84: TURNBULL GRIFFIN HAESLOOP ARCHITECTS (817 Bancroft Way, Berkeley, CA 94710; 510-841-9000; www.tgharchs.com)

pp. 1 (bottom center) and 42–49: CORNER/YOUNG ARCHITECTS, DONALD CORNER AND JENNY YOUNG (1062 E. 21st Ave., Eugene, OR 97405; 541-485-8861)

pp. 2, 5 (top), 13 (bottom), 133, 156, 161 (bottom), and 173: HUESTIS TUCKER ARCHITECTS, Jennifer Huestis, Principal in Charge (2349 Whitney Ave., Hamden, CT 06518; 203-248-1007)

pp. 3, 14 (bottom right), 15, 161 (top), 167, 174–181, 194–205, and 232: JAMES W. GIVENS DESIGN, 1059 Adams St., Eugene, OR 97402; 541-345-5053; jgivens@darkwing.uoregon.edu)

pp. 4 (left), 12 (bottom right), 30, 98, 99, 120–127, and 186–191: JACOBSON SILVERSTEIN WINSLOW ARCHITECTS, Max Jacobson, Partner in Charge (3106 Shattuck Ave., Berkeley, CA 94705; 510-848-8861; www.jswarch.com)

pp. 6, 9, 17 (top left), and 274–281: FERNAU & HARTMAN ARCHITECTS (2512 Ninth St., No. 2, Berkeley, CA 94710; 510-848-4480; www.fernauhartman.com)

pp. 8 and 85–88: ROSS CHAPIN ARCHITECTS (PO Box 230, 195 Second St., Langley, WA 98260; www.rosschapin.com; inquiry@rosschapin.com); Joy Moulton, owner/general contractor

pp. 10 (top), 137, 254, and 268–273: THE MILLER/HULL PARTNERSHIP, PROJECT TEAM: Craig Curtis and Sian Roberts (911 Western Ave., Rm. 220, Seattle, WA 98104; 206-682-6837; www.miller-hull.com)

pp. 10 (bottom), 22, 23, 26 (top), and 33–41: THE HENRY KLEIN PARTNERSHIP, ARCHITECTS (314 Pine St., Ste. 205, Mount Vernon, WA 98273; 360-336-2155; hkp@hkpa.com); landscape architect: Rich Haag & Associates

pp. 11 (top), 94–96, 134, and 183: CARNEY ARCHITECTS (215 S. King St., PO Box 9218, Jackson, WY 83002; 307-733-4000; www.carneyarchitects.com)

pp. 11 (bottom), 25, 51, 70, 71, 206, 224, 225, and 227–229: LAKE/FLATO ARCHITECTS, INC. (311 3rd St., #200, San Antonio, TX 78205; 210-227-3335; www.lakeflato.com)

pp. 12 (left), 16 (top right), 106, 107, 172, 207, 212–214, 237, 253, 255, 260, and 261: GEORGE HOMSEY ARCHITECT FAIA (500 Treat Ave., Suite 201, San Francisco, CA 94110; 415-285-9193)

pp. 13 (top), 128, 129 (top), 136, and 140–147: TURNBULL GRIFFIN HAESLOOP ARCHITECTS, Eric Haesloop, Partner in Charge (817 Bancroft Way, Berkeley, CA 94710; 510-841-9000; www.tgharchs.com)

pp. 14 (left), 230, and 240–245: DUANY PLATER-ZYBERK & CO., Andres Duany, Principal in Charge (1023 SW 25th Ave., Miami, FL 33135; 305-644-1023; www.dpz.com)

pp. 14 (top right), 77–79, 160, and 171: THALLON & EDRINGTON, ARCHITECTS: THALLON ARCHITECTURE (2303 McMorran, Eugene, OR 97403; 541-344-5210; thallonarch@continet.com) and David Edrington, Architect (240 W. 20th Ave., Eugene, OR 97405; 541-343-4383; edarchitect@qwest.net)

pp. 16 (bottom right), 110, 231, and 246–251: JOHN SILVERIO ARCHITECT (105 Proctor Rd., Lincolnville, ME 04849; 207-763-3885); Cindy Lang, Martinsville Vacation Rentals (207-372-8906; www.martinsvillemaine.com)

pp. 17 (top right and bottom), 24, 50, 52, 53, and 55–69: CASS CALDER SMITH ARCHITECTURE (44 McLea Court, San Francisco, CA 94103; 415-864-2800; www.ccs-architecture.com)

pp. 18–21, 29, 101, 155, 158, 168, and 208–210: JACOBSON SILVERSTEIN WINSLOW ARCHITECTS, Barbara Winslow, Partner in Charge (3106 Shattuck Ave., Berkeley, CA 94705; 510-848-8861; www.jswarch.com)

pp. 26 (bottom), 192, and 193: THALLON ARCHITECTURE WITH JAMES GIVENS DESIGN: THALLON ARCHITECTURE (2303 McMorran, Eugene, OR 97403; 541-344-5210; thallonarch@continet.com) and JAMES W. GIVENS DESIGN (1059 Adams St., Eugene, OR 97402; 541-345-5053; jgivens-@darkwing.uoregon.edu)

pp. 54, 154, 162–166, 238, and 239: JEFFERSON B. RILEY FAIA OF CENTERBROOK, CENTERBROOK ARCHITECTS AND PLANNERS (PO Box 955, Centerbrook, CT 06409; 860-767-0175)

p. 72: THE HENRY KLEIN PARTNERSHIP, ARCHITECTS (314 Pine St., Ste. 205, Mount Vernon, WA 98273; 360-336-2155; hkp@hkpa.com)

p. 73: JILL SOUSA ARCHITECT (2815 N. Lawrence, Tacoma, WA 98407; 253-469-9662; jillsousa@aol.com)

pp. 76, 109, and 170: BILL MASTIN, ARCHITECT (6633 Mokelumne Ave., Oakland, CA 94605; 510-562-4004)

pp. 89–92: C. A. TREADWELL ARCHITECTURE (853 Vallejo St., San Francisco, CA 94133; 415-362-3223)

pp. 97, 235, and 236: COTTLE GRAYBEAL YAW ARCHITECTS (PO Box 529, Basalt, CO 81621; 970-927-4925; www.cgyarchitects.com)

p. 103: MARC LAROCHE ARCHITECTS (181 Winslow Way, Ste. F, Bainbridge Island, WA 98110; 206-842-1366); Richard and Sheryl Vannelli, owners

p. 108: BATES ARCHITECTS (Box 510 Main St., Sag Harbor, NY 11963; 631-725-0229; www.batesmasi.com)

p. 111: ROBERT W. DU DOMAINE (1131 High Court, Berkeley, CA 94708; robwdd@hotmail.com)

pp. 112–118: TUT BARTZEN & ASSOCIATES (7 N. Monroe St., Richmond, VA 23220; 804-344-4405, 703-622-1950)

pp. 129 (bottom), 130, and 148–153: STUDIO B ARCHITECTS, Scott Lindenau (555 N. Mill St., Aspen, CO 81611; 970-920-9428; studiob@sopris.net; www.studiobarchitects.net)

p. 135: CHAD FLOYD FAIA OF CENTERBROOK, CENTERBROOK ARCHITECTS AND PLANNERS (PO Box 955, Centerbrook, CT 06409; 860-767-0175)

pp. 138, 139, 159, and 169: JEFFREY W. LIMERICK ARCHITECT (752 15th St., Boulder, CO 80302; 303-443-3266)

pp. 182, 184, and 185: GLENN ROBERT LYM ARCHITECT (59A Rodgers St., San Francisco, CA 94103; 415-621-4086; lym@lymarch.com)

p. 211: BERNIE BAKER ARCHITECT, PS (5571 Welfare Ave. NE, Bainbridge Island, WA 98110; 206-842-6278; bba@bainbridge.net)

pp. 233 (bottom) and 234: HUESTIS TUCKER ARCHITECTS, Bob Tucker, Principal in Charge (2349 Whitney Ave., Hamden, CT 06518; 203-248-1007)